Essays in Language, Translation, and the Digital Learning Technologies

in honour of Doug Thompson

Essays in Language, Translation, and the Digital Learning Technologies

in honour of Doug Thompson

edited by
George Talbot and Pamela Williams

Published by
Matador
12 Manor Walk, Coventry Road
Market Harborough
Leics LE16 9BP, UK
Tel: (+44) 1858 468828 / 469898
Fax: (+44) 1858 431649
Email: matador@troubador.co.uk
Web: www.troubador.co.uk/matador

ISBN 1 899293 67 1

Cover: Illustration by Pamela Williams, based on a detail of a sixteenth-century woodcut of Genoa harbour by Jacopo Philippo Bergomensis

Typesetting: Troubador Publishing Ltd, Market Harborough, UK
Printed and bound by Publish on Demand Ltd, Highbury Grove, London, UK

Matador is an imprint of Troubador Publishing Ltd

CONTENTS

CONTRIBUTORS

ANTHONY BALDRY is currently *Professore associato in Lingua e Traduzione – Lingua Inglese* at the Faculty of Medicine and Surgery, University of Pavia, and has taught English in many other Universities in Italy including Bologna, Chieti, and Milan in the past thirty years. Since the mid-eighties he has specialized in computer-assisted analysis of texts in English with reference to functional theories of language and has been involved in a number of Coimbra Group projects relating to distance learning. In recent years, he has specialized in the multimodal analysis of texts, publishing a successful collection of articles (*Multimodality and Multimediality in the Distance-learning Age*). In so doing he has channelled many of the above research interests into web-based projects relating to the development of multimodal corpora of film texts and their analysis through multimodal concordancing techniques.

PATRICK CORNESS was formerly Principal Lecturer in Russian and German at Coventry University and he is a member of the Technology-Enhanced Language Learning (TELL) Consortium. His main interests are in translation, with particular reference to Slavonic languages. He collaborates with the Institute of Translation Studies at Charles University, Prague, and the Department of Computational Linguistics at Vytautas Magnus University, Kaunas. Recent publications include 'Stylistic Aspects of Translation from Czech into English', in *Issues of Translation into a Non-native Language: Folia Translatologica*, vol. 7, ed. Patrick Corness and Jana Králová, Charles University, Prague, 1999; 'Multiconcord: A Tool for Cross-Linguistic Research', in *Lexis in Contrast*, ed. Bengt Altenberg and Sylviane Granger, John Benjamins, 2001 (forthcoming). He is currently working on a translation of a novel by the Polish writer Witold Gombrowicz.

ALESSANDRO GENTILI is Resident Director of the James Madison University Semester in Florence. Formerly Assistant Lecturer in Italian at University College Cork and Head of Italian at the British Institute of Florence, he has edited *The Green Flame* (with Catherine O'Brien), *I diari di Stephen Spender*, and *Rosa di macchia: antologia di poesia irlandese dopo Yeats*, as well as translating two collections of John Montague's poems, *Il quaderno smarrito* and *Il campo abbandonato.*

PATRICK LEECH is a full-time researcher at the Department of Translation, Language and Cultural Studies at the University of Bologna. He is currently working on the history of 'plain style' in seventeenth- and eighteenth-century theories of language.

BRIAN McCARTHY is Head of the Modern Languages Program at the University of Wollongong, Australia. His research interests are foreign language teaching methodology, computer-assisted language learning, software development, phonetics, and translation.

MARINA ORSINI-JONES is Subject Leader for Italian at Coventry University. She has been involved in computer-assisted language learning for many years and has published a CD-ROM to teach Italian language and society and various articles on CALL. She has also published in the field of contemporary Italian studies with reference to immigrant women in Italy.

ANNALISA SANDRELLI is a graduate of the *Scuola Superiore di Lingue Moderne per Interpreti e Traduttori* of the University of Trieste. Between 1996 and 1998 she was Lector in Italian at the University of Hull. In 1999 she was awarded a Fellowship for a research project on simultaneous interpreting, under the Marie Curie Training and Mobility of Researchers programme of the European Commission. Her main research interests and publications are in the areas are interpreting (conference and liaison) and film translation (both subtitling and dubbing).

FEDERICA SCARPA is Associate Professor of English Translation at the SSLMIT, University of Trieste. Her main research interests focus on specialized translation (social sciences, law, and information technology) and computer-assisted terminography. She is currently involved in a project on the academic language of migration studies, both in English and Italian. Her recent publications include: *La traduzione specializzata. Lingue speciali e mediazione linguistica*, 2001, and *Manuale di terminologia* (edited with M. Magris, M. T. Musacchio, and L. Rega), 2002, both published by Hoepli, Milan. Since 1995 she is editor of *Rivista internazionale di tecnica della traduzione/International Journal of Translation* (EUT: Trieste).

GEORGE TALBOT is a Senior Lecturer in Italian and Head of the Department of Modern Languages at the University of Hull. Among his books are *Montale's 'mestiere vile'*, *Montale: Words in Time*, a volume of essays edited along with Doug Thompson, an edition of *Selected Poems* by Eugenio Montale, and a critical edition of *Lord Charlemont's History of Italian Poetry from Dante to Metastasio.*

INTRODUCTION

This book brings together nine essays on the themes of language, translation, and digital learning technologies, written by friends and colleagues of Doug Thompson on the occasion of his retirement.

The essays reflect his own interdisciplinary interests, which have ranged from Dante studies to translation and the integration of new technologies into the process of learning language.

George Talbot
Pamela Williams

A GENEALOGY OF TERMINOLOGY: JOHN LOCKE'S *ESSAY CONCERNING HUMAN UNDERSTANDING**

Patrick Leech
University of Bologna

The study of terminology, whether this is regarded as a fully-fledged discipline or merely as a practice, would appear to be a recent phenomenon. According to one commentator, it began to emerge as a mature theoretical reality only in the twentieth century; for another, it was still only 'gradually gaining ground' in the late 1990s.[1] In a wider sense, however, the study of terminology, the 'field of activity concerned with the collection, description, processing and presentation of terms', has of course a much longer history.[2] Alain Rey has noted how a concern with using language to name separate objects in a single field was central both to Linnaeus' classification of the plant world, and to Diderot's plea for greater standardization of language in the work of artisans. Early encyclopaedic dictionaries were also informed by the same desire to plot areas of knowledge through the study of terminology.[3] Little has been done to explore the growth of terminology and terminography from the point of view of the linguist or the historian of terminology, rather than that of a historian of science.[4] Even less has been done to trace the history of a theoretical assumption crucial to the activity of terminology: the notion of the active part the scientist or terminologist can play in the assigning of terms to objects, whether man-made or natural.

*I would like to thank Michele Gardini, Derek Boothman, George Talbot, and Pamela Williams for their comments on this paper.

This active role for the scientist in naming the objects under consideration is an endeavour which may now seem innocent, but which may once have been seen as Promethean, at least, or heretical, at worst. It was once accepted that the objects of the natural world were given names by Adam, as recounted in Genesis, and that as this happened before the Fall, these must have been the 'true' names of the species.[5] The idea that scientists could have the freedom to name the objects of their study, it will argued here, was given a particularly clear formulation in the philosophy of John Locke, and in particular in the third book of his *Essay Concerning Human Understanding* (1690), entitled 'Of Words'.[6] Although Locke nowhere treats the specific problem of the uses of terminology within a related field, his theorizing of the possibilities and demands of scientific discourse, and in particular the problems involved in the relation between term, idea, and object, may constitute a relevant genealogy to the study of terminology.

The moving spirit behind Locke's epistemology as formulated in his *Essay Concerning Human Understanding* was the climate of scientific exploration in late seventeenth-century England. In his 'Epistle to the Reader', Locke made an explicit reference to this context of a 'Commonwealth of Learning' and its 'Master-Builders, whose mighty Designs, in advancing the Sciences, will leave lasting Monuments to the Admiration of Posterity'. Not everyone, however, could aspire to be 'a *Boyle* or a *Sydenham*' or the 'incomparable Mr *Newton*'. His own role, instead, was to be that of 'an Under-Labourer in clearing the Ground a little, and removing some of the Rubbish, that lies in the way to Knowledge'. Questions of terminology were crucial to this work: the rubbish consisted, in particular, of the 'learned but frivolous use of uncouth, affected or unintelligible Terms, introduced into the Sciences'. Thus there was a need to expose 'vague and insignificant forms of speech and abuse of language', an intention which was at the heart of his work.[7]

One way in which this could be done was to operate a clear distinction between common and scientific language, between what he called 'civil' and 'philosophical' uses of words (III, ix, 3). Whereas common use '*regulates the meanings of Words* pretty well for common Conversation', it was not sufficient for philosophical or scientific discourse, 'there being scarce any Name, of any very complex *Idea* [...] which, in common Use, has not a great latitude, and which, keeping within the bounds of Propriety, may not be made the sign of far different *Ideas*' (III, ix, 8).[8] The vagueness of reference in civil use thus resulted in the need for careful definition in scientific discourse: 'it is sometimes necessary for the ascertaining of the signification of Words, to *declare their Meaning*; where either common Use has left it uncertain or loose; [...] or where the Term [...] is liable to any Doubtfulness or Mistake' (III, xi, 12).

This concern for careful consideration of the meaning of terms can be linked to the growth of a scientific discourse whose chief pragmatic principle has been considered one of 'maximum transparency'.[9] Locke has thus been seen as operating alongside Bacon, Hobbes, and the Royal Society within a 'plain style' tradition, one of whose principal characteristics was a 'fear of metaphor'.[10] However, while the 'abuses' of language Locke indicated here did include 'artificial and figurative applications of Words' (III, x, 33), elsewhere he makes some highly pertinent comments on the use of metaphor in the construction of human knowledge.[11] Moreover, if Locke's preoccupation was with transparency, it should be remembered that he was aware of the ultimate impossibility of this goal, given the inherent 'imperfections' of language. Although language was 'the great Conduit, whereby Men convey their Discoveries, Reasonings, and Knowledge from one to another' (III, xi, 5), it was also true that 'the very nature of Words, makes it almost unavoidable for many of them to be doubtful and uncertain in their significations' (III, ix, 1). Obstacles to transparency were abuses such as exaggerated rhetoric or inconstancy of use. But there were also, for Locke, problems which concerned much more wide-ranging problems of reference and signification, and it is his discussion of these problems which is of most interest in the context of the study of terminology.

In particular, for Locke, there were certain common misunderstandings about the nature of words and their reference to the human and natural world. One of these misunderstandings was the common assumption that words referred not only to the ideas of the speaker but also to '*the* Ideas *in the Minds also of other Men, with whom they communicate*' (III, ii, 4). The danger here was that the 'common acceptation' of the signification of a word was no guarantee of a real shared idea. Hence the need, as a remedy, for the definition and open comparison of the signification of a term in scientific discourse, as we have seen. A second, and much more dangerous misunderstanding, without which there could be no guarantee of real communication, the transmission of the same idea from one mind to another through speech,[12] stemmed from the vanity of men: 'Because Men would not be thought to talk *barely* of their own Imaginations, but of Things as they really are; therefore they *often suppose their Words to stand also for the reality of Things*' (III, ii, 5). Locke is insistent that words do not refer to things, but rather to the ideas of things in the minds of men.[13] Words 'signify nothing but the ideas that are in the mind of the speaker', and: 'it is a perverting the use of Words, and brings unavoidable Obscurity and Confusion into their Signification, whenever we make them stand for anything, but those *Ideas* we have in our own Minds' (III, ii, 5).

This insistence that words refer to ideas of things rather than things themselves is crucial to the subsequent development of scientific practice and at the basis also of the study of terminology, whose foundation is the conventional, agreed act of naming objects and actions within a defined system, a field of human knowledge. The historical context in which Locke was writing was the neo-Platonist tradition in which there was assumed to be an original, natural (but now lost) connection between word and thing, an assumed original Adamic language from which the actual languages of the seventeenth-century were derived.[14] Locke, instead, in a glorious flourish of confident individualism and humanism, accords the naming power of Adam to every individual: 'The same Liberty also, that *Adam* had of affixing any new name to any *Idea*; the same has any one still, [...] but only with this difference, that in Places, where Men in Society have already established a Language amongst them, the significations of Words are very warily and sparingly to be alter'd' (III, vi, 51). The absolute Adamic freedom in naming that Locke accords to the individual is quickly tempered by some social realism, but it may be supposed that no such limitations would fence in those working in the exciting new fields of scientific discovery. This power of naming the objects of study in the human or natural world, however, emerges only through a careful consideration of the problems concerning the precise significations of words, the principal object of the central chapters of the third book of Locke's *Essay*.

In his chapter 'On the Names of Mixed Modes and Relations', Locke makes a crucial distinction, in language and in our knowledge of and communication about the things of the world, between what he calls *mixed modes* and *substances*. The latter he takes to be ideas about things really existing in the physical world, although Locke is radically opposed to the notion that things in the real world conform to stable general types or species. He discusses the problem of reference to substances in a later chapter. For the moment, however, Locke is content to argue that in terms for these cases, there is the 'Supposition of some real Being, from which they are taken, and to which they are conformable' (III, v, 3). Mixed modes, on the other hand, differ from the ideas of substances in the sense that there is no supposition of real physical existence. The words used to refer to mixed modes '*terminate in the* Idea that is in the Mind, and lead not the Thoughts any farther' (III, iv, 2). Mixed modes are formed by the combination of single distinct ideas, binding them together to create new, more complex ones. One of the examples Locke takes is the term 'murder', formed by the combination of the simple ideas of 'killing' and 'man'. Locke stresses that this combination is arbitrary in the sense that there is no such thing as 'murder' in the natural world, but only in the (arbitrary) combination, in the minds of men, of the ideas 'man' and 'killing'. The term 'murder', in fact, is applicable when a man kills a man, but not when a man kills a sheep, although there is no reason to be found in nature why the idea of 'man' rather than that of 'sheep' should be combined with the idea of 'killing' to form a distinct complex idea: 'For what greater connection in Nature, has the *Idea* of a Man, than the *Idea* of a Sheep, with Killing, that this is made a particular Species of Action, signified by the word *Murder*, and the other not?' (III, v, 6).

The liberty that man has in combining different ideas to form new ones (and marking these ideas with terms) is crucial to Locke's epistemology. Terms such as 'murder' indicate human phenomena which do not conform to categories pre-existing in nature but signify instead 'nothing but the abstract *Ideas* in the Mind, to which the Name is annexed' (III, v, 1). The fact that these complex ideas are the work of men, acting in total freedom (in theory at least) to combine any different single ideas to form new, combined, or mixed ones, is evidence of Locke's radically constructivist approach to human knowledge. Mixed modes, what would now be considered the cultural categories defining and regulating human behaviour, are '*made by the Understanding*' (III, v, 2).[15]

The following paragraphs will discuss how Locke develops this constructivist epistemology in the far more controversial area of natural phenomena. Here it is enough to point out that the combination of simple ideas to form higher complex ideas or mixed modes involves a cognitive activity which may be familiar to students of terminology. The process by which complex ideas are formed, according to Locke, is three-fold: 'first, [the mind] chuses a certain Number. Secondly, It gives them connexion, and makes them into one *Idea*. Thirdly, It ties them together by a Name' (III, v, 4). Terminology, then, is part of the active construction of human knowledge, the term being seen as a functional element in the construction and preservation of a certain concept. The term, in other words, acts as a sort of 'pro-memoria', a signpost to a complex idea, and is necessary precisely because these concepts, not pre-existing in nature and composed of different simple ideas, are man-made and thus to a certain extent fragile:

> For the connexion between the loose parts of those complex *Ideas* being made by the Mind, this union, which has no particular foundation in Nature, would cease again, were there not something that did, as it were, hold it together, and keep the parts from scattering. Though therefore it be the Mind that makes the Collection, 'tis the Name which is, as it were the Knot, that ties them fast together. (III, v, 10)

The term, or the 'name' as Locke calls it, is thus a 'knot' which aids recall and ensures that phenomena which are encountered a second time can be classified according to the categories of knowledge freely-formed on a previous occasion. Terminology, it would seem, is in a sense the key to human understanding.

Locke's view of the constructivist nature of human understanding is further developed in the following chapter, 'Of the Names of Substances'. Here Locke is concerned to take his notion of the reference of words to human ideas of things rather than to things themselves into the heart of the battle against the Aristotelian doctrine of the essential division of the natural world into fixed types or species.[16] He sees ideas of substances, like mixed modes, as complex ideas, created through the combination of simple ideas. Thus the complex idea of the substance 'gold' is made by combining the simple ideas of 'shining yellow', 'weight', 'fusibility', 'malleability', and so on (III, ii, 3).[17] For Locke, then, there are no pre-existing natural essences, but only plural and individual physical entities which the human mind sorts into general categories (ideas) for its own use. Thus: '*General and Universal* belong not to the real existence of Things, but *are the Inventions and Creatures of the Understanding*, made by it for its own use, *and concern only Signs*, whether Words or Ideas' (III, iii, 11).[18] The term 'sun', for example, does not refer to any unchanging species in nature, but instead can be distinguished from the term 'star' solely by reason of the position of the observer, for 'each fixed Star would answer the *Idea* the name *Sun* stands for, to one who were placed in a due distance' and thus 'that might be a Sun to one, which is a Star to another' (III, vi, 1). Essence, then, does not pre-exist in nature, but is instead an idea. Locke argues that: 'The measure and boundary of each Sort, or *Species*, whereby it is constituted that particular Sort and distinguished from others, is that we call its *Essence*, which *is* nothing but that *abstract* Idea *to which the Name is annexed*' (III, vi, 2).

Thus the categories into which the natural world is divided, like the human phenomena discussed in his chapter on mixed modes, can also be found in the mind, rather than in nature. The essences Locke talks of here are not real, pre-existing forms but 'nominal essences', a concept which Locke keeps separate from the notion of 'real essences'. As regards the latter, Locke positions himself in the tradition of radical scepticism: 'as to the real *Essences* of Substances, we only suppose their Being, without precisely knowing what they are' (III, vi, 6).[19] We cannot, says Locke, rank or class things in the natural world by their real essences because, in an absolute sense, 'we know them not': 'There is not so contemptible a Plant or Animal, that does not confound the most inlarged Understanding' (III, vi, 9). This being the case, the classification of the world into sorts is a human activity of setting the boundaries, of providing what might be called a 'working definition' or standard to which substances in the real world can be compared. Thus the term 'gold' is defined by the limits or boundaries set up by men with regard to its constitution. What substances can be classed as gold becomes a human problem to be solved by measuring a particular, really existing body against a set of defining criteria (a precise colour and weight, with the properties of malleability, fusibility, and solubility in *acqua regia*) which are man-made (see III, vi, 6). Locke gives as an illustration of this problem also the arduous labour of the chemist, when samples of 'sulphur, antimony or vitriol' turn out to 'betray Qualities so different one from another, as to frustrate the Expectation and Labour of very wary Chymists'. If things in nature were really divided into fixed species, then 'it would be as impossible to find different Properties in any two individual Substances of the same *Species*, as it is to find different Properties in two Circles, or two equilateral Triangles' (III, vi, 8). Nominal essence, then, being a man-made entity imposed on an ultimately unknowable real essence, must be a cognitively constructed category, an essence which exists in the social and negotiated world of human society and language.

Locke's concept of nominal essence is thus a crucial part of his attempt to destroy the bases for natural, pre-existing species independent of human understanding, the supposition that there could be 'precise and unmovable boundaries' of species (III, vi, 8). Essence being nominal, not real, it is precisely the act of naming which cuts up and categorizes the natural world, setting the boundaries for the human conceptions of really existing things. Thus: 'the *Species of Things to us are nothing but the ranking of them under distinct* Names, *according to the complex* Ideas *in us*; and not according to precise, distinct, real Essences in them' (III, vi, 8). In the human understanding of the natural world, too, terminology, the ranking of things 'under distinct Names', is the key to knowledge.

Locke's radically constructivist stance towards human knowledge, based on his desire to be an 'under-labourer' in the service of science, reorients the activity of the scientist away from the 'discovery' of essences that pre-exist in the world towards the active taxonomy of notions and really existing individual substances according to a human understanding based on the combination of specific ideas. This taxonomy is necessarily a terminological activity, also in the precise sense of fixing boundaries, of deciding (or *determining*) the extension of a specific complex idea, in other words where its reference *terminates*.[20] This new conception of the scope and nature of scientific activity thus reserves a substantial place for terminology, conceived of as an active, constructive cognitive science.

It has been argued in this chapter that terminology has an important genealogy in the work of John Locke, in particular in his anti-essentialist stance in epistemology and in the consequent constructivism and prescriptivism associated with the giving of names to ideas denoting both abstract notions (mixed modes) and naturally occurring objects (substances). Part of the work of terminologists consists in the review of the notions and terms current in a given scientific or technical field, and thus in an extensive and accurate survey of use. Little scope is given for inventing new words: denominations for concepts have to coincide with word-forms 'used by the specialists when referring to a concept of a given notional structure'.[21] This aspect of their work is predominantly descriptive. Studies of terminology, however, also have an important prescriptive side to them. Terminologists take note of the different forms which can be used to refer to a given concept, but their task is also to award priority to a single term, and thus to 'fix terminological units as standardized forms'.[22] They make recommendations for preferring one particular term 'over other terms which may have been used to describe the same concept in the past' (and similarly, for prohibiting or discouraging the use of alternative forms with the same denotation).[23] The ultimate goal of the terminologist is thus the systematizing of terms already in use in current scientific and technical discourse. This act of creating order and system out of the chaos of use in many different technical and scientific contexts is an important nominalist activity, even if it does not involve the actual creation of neologisms. As a prescriptive activity, it relies, moreover, on a consensual theory of denotation. In this sense, it has been argued that the prescriptivism of terminology, involving as it does the construction of glossaries and term banks by means of 'close collaboration between terminologists and subject specialists',[24] is the result of a wider search for consensus than lexicographical prescriptivism, often based solely on the 'criteria of a given academic body'.[25] As Locke pointed out, if terms are not to denote merely the ideas that the speaker has in mind, but common, shared ideas in the minds of both speaker and hearer, it may be necessary to 'declare their meaning' (III, xi, 12). The terminologists' glossaries or term banks can represent precisely this consensual declaration of meaning, a real contract between parties,[26] in particular when these terms and their definitions are given institutional legitimacy and thus a regulative and standardizing function, as with the ISO.[27]

The knowledge and activity of the terminologist is an eminently practical one, aiming at the 'achievement of accurate, modern and unambiguous professional communication'.[28] Locke was similarly modest about his aim, which was not to know all things but only 'those which concern our conduct'.[29] But this activity, which from the outside may appear to be merely the arid work of an under-labourer in the service of the description of things, is in fact one which plays a vital role in the creation, classification, and dissemination of human knowledge, and one which is to be collocated firmly within a conventionalist and constructivist approach to language.

NOTES

1 J. Sager, *A Practical Guide to Terminology Processing* (Amsterdam-Philadelphia: John Benjamins, 1990), pp. 1–2; M. T. Cabré, 'Terminology today', in *Terminology, LSP and Translation. Studies in Language Engineering in Honour of Juan Sager*, ed. H. Somers (Amsterdam-Philadelphia: John Benjamins, 1996), pp. 15–33 (p. 15).

2 Sager, *A Practical Guide to Terminology Processing*, p. 1.

3 A. Rey, 'Origins and Development of Terminology', in *Essays on Terminology*, transl. and ed. J. Sager (Amsterdam-Philadelphia: John Benjamins, 1995), pp. 11–22 (pp. 13–14). See also M. Foucault, *The Order of Things. An Archaeology of the Human Sciences* (New York: Random House, 1970), especially Chapter 5.

4 Exceptions are Rey, 'Origins and Development'; J. C. Boulanger, 'Les onomastiques égyptiens au temps des pharaons', in *Terminology, LSP and Translation*, pp. 83–98. See also M. M. Slaughter's important book, *Universal Languages and Scientific Taxonomy in the Seventeenth Century* (Cambridge: Cambridge University Press, 1982).

5 For a discussion of this, see R. Harris and T. J. Taylor, *Landmarks in Linguistic Thought. The Western Tradition from Socrates to Saussure* (London-New York: Routledge, 1989), Chapter 3.

6 John Locke, *An Essay Concerning Human Understanding* [1690], ed. P. Nidditch (Oxford: Oxford University Press, 1975). Subsequent references to Locke's *Essay* will be made in the text, indicating the relevant book, chapter, and section.

7 'The Epistle to the Reader', pp. 9–10.

8 A. C. Baugh and T. Cable, *A History of the English Language*, 4th edn. (London: Routledge, 1993), who assert that Locke 'wished that the qualities desired for scientific prose could be extended to all prose' (p. 250).

9 M. Gotti, *Robert Boyle and the Language of Science* (Milan: Guerini, 1996), p. 21.

10 See, for example, G. Lakoff and M. Johnson, *Metaphors We Live By* (Chicago-London: Chicago University Press, 1980), pp. 189–92, and B. Vickers, *Storia della retorica* (Bologna: Il Mulino, 1994), pp. 262–64. For discussions of the 'plain style' tradition in scientific discourse, see in particular R. F. Jones, 'Science and English Prose Style in the Third Quarter of the Seventeenth Century', *PMLA*, 15 (1930), 977–1009, and R. K. Merton, *Science, Technology and Society in Seventeenth Century England* (New York: Howard Fertig, 1979), pp. 19–22. See also the criticisms of Jones and Merton in R. Kroll, 'Introduction', in *Philosophy, Science and Religion in England 1640–1799*, eds. R. Kroll, R. Ashcraft, and P. Zagorin (Cambridge: Cambridge University Press, 1992), pp. 1–28, and R. Kroll, *The Material Word. Literate Culture in the Restoration and Early Eighteenth Century* (Baltimore: Johns Hopkins University Press, 1991), pp. 1–2. For the prose style of the Royal Society, see F. Christensen, 'John Wilkins and the Royal Society's Reform of Prose Style', in *John Wilkins and 17th Century British Linguistics*, ed. J. L. Subbiondo (Amsterdam-Philadelphia: John Benjamins, 1992), pp. 133–52; L. Formigari, *Language and Experience in Seventeenth-Century British Philosophy* (Amsterdam-Philadelphia: John Benjamins, 1988), pp. 52–61; S. Shapin and S. Shaffer, *Leviathan and the Air Pump. Hobbes, Boyle and the Experimental Life* (Princeton, NJ: Princeton University Press, 1985), pp. 66–78; Gotti, *Robert Boyle and the Language of Science*, pp. 23–27.

11 In particular, Locke notes the ways in which language used to describe phenomena pertaining to the senses takes on metaphorical uses: 'It may also lead us a little towards the Original of all our Notions and Knowledge, if we remark, how great a dependence our *Words* have on common sensible *Ideas*; and how those, which are made use of to stand for Actions and Notions quite removed from sense *have their rise from thence, and from obvious*

sensible Ideas *are transferred to more abstruse significations*, and made to stand for *Ideas* that come not under the cognizance of our senses; e.g. to *Imagine, Apprehend, Comprehend, Adhere, Conceive, Instil, Disgust, Disturbance, Tranquillity*, etc. are all Words taken from the Operations of sensible Things and applied to certain Modes of Thinking' (III, i, 5). Although Locke does not use the term 'metaphor', here, the extension of reference from one sphere of meaning to another is a clearly metaphorical process. For the importance of this passage for eighteenth-century interpreters, see H. Aarsleff, 'Locke's Influence', in *The Cambridge Companion to Locke*, ed. V. Chapell (Cambridge: Cambridge University Press, 1994), pp. 252–89 (pp. 272–73). For metaphor in Locke's writings, see S. H. Clark, '"The Whole Internal World His Own": Locke and Metaphor Reconsidered', *Journal of the History of Ideas*, 59 (1998), 241–65; V. Brown, 'The "Figure" of God and the Limits to Liberalism: A Rereading of Locke, *Essay* and *Two Treatises*', *Journal of the History of Ideas*, 60 (1999), 83–100.

12 This model of language, as essentially the transferring of an idea in the speaker's mind to the mind of the hearer, has been termed 'telementation' by R. Harris. See his *Language, Saussure and Wittgenstein. How to Play Games with Words* (London-New York: Routledge, 1988), pp. 99 ff.

13 Locke's notion that words refer to ideas rather than things was not entirely original. In the debates on language in the seventeenth century, this notion can be found, for example, in the writings of Seth Ward, George Dalgarno. and Richard Burthogge (see Formigari, *Language and Experience*, pp. 22, 70–71, 102). Paul Guyer argues for the influence of the Dutch emigré Franco Burgerdijk in this context ('Locke's Philosophy of Language', in *The Cambridge Companion to Locke*, pp. 115–145), whereas other claims have been made for the more general influence of the anti-Cartesian Pierre Gassendi – M. J. Osler, 'The Intellectual Sources of Robert Boyle's Philosophy of Nature: Gassendi's Voluntarism and Boyle's Physico-Theological Project', in *Philosophy, Science and Religion in England*, pp. 178–98.

14 The notion that man could get back to the original Adamic language was a feature of a number of Protestant mystics and Platonists from John Amos Comenius and Jakob Boehme to Thomas Vaughan and his Manifesto (1652) of 'Rosicrucian Linguistics'. See Formigari, *Language and Experience*, pp. 17–18; H. Aarsleff, 'Jacob Boehme' and 'Comenius', in *Dictionary of Scientific Biography*, 16 vols, ed. C. Coulston Gillespie (New York: Charles Scribner' Sons, 1971–73), vol. II, pp. 222–23, and vol. III, pp. 359–63. These proponents of the return to a natural Adamic language were one of the principal targets of John Wilkins' *Essay Towards a Real Character and a Philosophical Language* (1666), whose intention was to 'repair the ruins of Babel' through the imposition of an arbitrary nomenclature – see H. Aarsleff, *From Locke to Saussure. Essays on the Study of Language and Intellectual History* (London: Athlone, 1982), pp. 239–77; Formigari, *Language and Experience*, pp. 68–89; U. Eco, *La ricerca della lingua perfetta nella cultura europea* (Bari: Laterza, 1993), pp. 255–78. Wilkins shared with Comenius and others, however, the belief that a nomenclature could provide an exhaustive inventory of the phenomena of the natural world (see Formigari, *Language and Experience*, p. 82, and also the position of Locke as outlined below). For universal language schemes in the seventeenth century, see also V. Salmon, *The Works of Francis Lodwick. A Study of his Writings in the Intellectual Context of the Seventeenth Century* (London: Longman, 1972), pp. 12–42.

15 We may note that Locke's constructivism takes the inquirer into human understanding into the realms of comparative anthropology, comparative linguistics, and, indeed, translation. For given that men are free to combine ideas in this way and thus also to coin new ones, their actions in this manner will be such as to create new and distinct areas of human knowledge and behaviour, what we would now call cultures: 'it being so obvious to observe great store of *Words in one* Language *which have not any that answer them in another*. Which plainly shews that those of one Country, by their customs and manner of Life, have found occasion to make several complex Ideas, and give names to them, which others never collected into specific *Ideas*' (III, v, 8). In Locke, as Hans Aarsleff has argued, can be found the seeds of the Romantic notion of the characteristic differences in the thought and cultures of different peoples speaking different languages (*From Locke to Saussure*, pp. 27–28, 344; 'Locke's influence', pp. 274–76). See also S. V. Land, *The Philosophy of Language in Britain.*

Major Theories from Hobbes to Thomas Reid (New York: AMS Press, 1986), p. 54.

16 See Slaughter, *Universal Languages and Scientific Taxonomy*, Chapter 1.

17 For concise explications of Locke's theory of ideas with regard to substances, see Land, *The Philosophy of Language in Britain*, pp. 43–51, and Slaughter, *Universal Languages and Scientific Taxonomy*, pp. 198–207.

18 It is this move by Locke from the particular and individual nature of *things* ('All Things, that exist, being Particulars', III, iii, 1) to general *ideas* which was rejected by Berkeley, for whom ideas, too, were always particular (see Guyer, 'Locke's Philosophy of Language', p. 127). See also Land, *The Philosophy of Language in Britain*, pp. 86–91. Elsewhere (p. 19 ff.), Land points out that Berkeley's position was prefigured in Hobbes' radical nominalism and denial of universals. The importance of Berkeley's critique is that it frees the analysis of language from concerns of referentiality and opens up the way to pragmatic analysis. For Berkeley, according to Lia Formigari, 'universality [...] is not a quality but a function' (*Language and Experience*, p. 129).

19 See Robert Boyle's similar notion of form being only the 'denominating state of matter' (Formigari, *Language and Experience*, p. 111; see also Osler, 'The Intellectual Sources of Robert Boyle's Philosophy of Nature', pp. 186–87) and his scepticism regarding the possibility of knowing the real essence of any natural substance (Gotti, *Robert Boyle and the Language of Science*, p. 36). Hans Aarsleff (*From Locke to Saussure*, pp. 12–13) has pointed out a similar scepticism regarding the knowability of things, given that they can only be perceived through their external manifestations, in Marin Mersenne's *La Vérité des Sciences* (1625).

20 See Rey, 'Origins and Development of Terminology', pp. 15–16.

21 Cabré, 'Terminology Today', p. 25; see also M. T. Cabré, *Terminology: Theory, Methods and Applications* (Amsterdam-Philadelphia: John Benjamins, 1998), p. 51.

22 Cabré, 'Terminology Today', p. 26.

23 J. Pearson, *Terms in Context* (Amsterdam-Philadelphia: John Benjamins, 1998), p. 22. Thus the ISO standardization guide advises not only the prescription of terms to use but also proscription of 'deprecated terms' used to refer to the same concept (see Pearson, p. 23 and Sager, *A Practical Course in Terminology Processing*, p. 151). Sager, however, appears to err on the side of modesty with regard to the prescriptivism of terminology studies, arguing that 'dictionaries and term banks, unless they have a language planning function with appropriate powers, have no influence on the standardisation of terms', although he concedes that 'term banks may exercise a strong harmonising influence on usage' (p. 116).

24 Sager, *A Practical Course in Terminology Processing*, p. 22. See here Robert Boyle's awareness of the need for consent by scientists over the reference of terms (see Gotti, *Robert Boyle and the Language of Science*, p. 30).

25 Cabré, 'Terminology Today', p. 26.

26 Roy Harris describes as 'contractualist' theories of language which emphasize arbitrary convention and agreement over meaning. His formulation indicates the links between this approach and Lockean anti-essentialism: 'Linguistic knowledge, for the contractualist, does not reach out to the structure of reality; it is simply knowledge of what the contract is, *The Language Makers* (London: Duckworth, 1980), p. 105. There would appear to be a clear link here, between the constructivism of Locke's epistemology and approach to language and the contractualism of his politics.

27 See the discussion on standardization in Pearson, *Terms in Context*, pp. 22–24.

28 Cabré, 'Terminology Today', p. 26.

29 Quoted in P. Hazard, *The European Mind 1680–1715*, transl. J. Lewis May (London: Penguin, 1964), p. 283.

TOWARDS AN ACCOUNT OF DANTE'S RECEPTION IN THE EUROPEAN ENLIGHTENMENT

George Talbot
University of Hull

Each generation of the twentieth century produced a new survey of Dante in English, beginning with Paget Toynbee's *Dante in English Literature: From Chaucer to Cary*.[1] Roderick Marshall, accepting what he found in Toynbee, took up the tale a generation later in his *Italy in English Literature 1755–1815* and broadened the scope to other Italian high literature.[2] Werner Friedrich in *Dante's Fame Abroad, 1350–1850* (1950) presented half a millennium of influence, at an historical remove of a century, again taking up much of what he found in Toynbee and Marshall.[3] Peter Brand dealt with Dante among others, and their relationship to the English Romantics,[4] and then, around 1965, as might have been foreseen, there followed a deluge of material on Dante in English, including William de Sua's survey, Harry McWilliam's article on the Irish contribution, and Gilbert Cunningham's summing up of fifty years of such activity, his two-volume *The Divine Comedy in English: A Critical Bibliography* (1965–66).[5] The process continued in Robin Kirkpatrick's *English and Italian Literature*, towards the end of the century.[6]

These books are all noble and useful pieces of scholarship belonging to their respective generations, and I have no intention of denigrating any of them. Specifically in relation to Dante, however, despite occasional new departures, there is an unhelpful degree of repetition. Given the terrain, some repetition is inevitable. But uncritical repetition is dangerous. Even the most compendious of bibliographical studies is prone to errors and omissions. The temptation of those following in the shadow of mighty tomes such as those of Toynbee or Cunningham is to accept the data at face value, rather than to return to the archives or indeed to seek out new sources. And this has led to a recycling of errors and prolonged neglect of significant primary materials. A further criticism which might be urged against these books relates to the issues of reception and influence, and it is the charge that they are often theoretically naive. For example, individual translations are dismissed as 'poor' or 'quaint', without an attempt to engage in what, following Clifford Geertz, we have learned to call 'thick interpretation'.[7] That is to say, they fail to engage in the wider questions of the day concerning the assumptions of individual translators and their original audiences. Ultimately, a 'thick interpretation' of Dante's significance for the Enlightenment mind is the aim of my project, although along the way there will be any amount of empirical word crunching of forgotten and indeed previously unknown translations, as well as more rarefied theory. The age of digital resources provides several useful techniques for us to enhance our local knowledge of Dante reception through the medium of translation. One such translation – the first complete one – is now scarcely known, though in its day Henry Boyd's version drew William Blake and John Flaxman to Dante and, in both cases, to the necessity of learning Italian to read him.

What tools then might the present generation bring to the study of Dante's *fortuna*? Firstly, contemporary studies are likely to be influenced by the current prestige of Historicism, and secondly, it would be rash to ignore the digital revolution which is around us. However, any worthwhile account of Dante's influence on European culture requires us to dwell on some reception theory and some documentary evidence from the historical record. Reception Theory is dominated by modes of thinking derived directly or indirectly from the philosophy of Hegel, ways of thinking foreign to most of us who have grown up across the water from continental Europe. It was not always so. T. S. Eliot's well-known essay on 'Tradition and the Individual Talent' taps into that source and presents us with an Idealist account of the power of re-interpretation which a later work may possess in relation to a work written centuries before, and perhaps long forgotten.[8] Ezra Pound's near fetishization of Guido Cavalcanti is such an example of an obsessive modernist artist living out that philosophy. The Modernists' re-appropriation of the *Stilnovisti* is an example of what Walter Benjamin dubbed the *Nachleben* (the afterlife) of a text or body of texts.[9] And it is this concept of an afterlife – so pregnant with significance in the case of Dante's *Commedia* – which carries so much force for reception theorists.

It is easy to forget that the *Commedia*'s afterlife was slumber-filled for a couple of centuries after the Council of Trent. And any attempt to explain a revival must also address the question of why a text was set aside in the first place – but that is not the main burden of this essay. Before passing on from Reception Theory, it is instructive to cite its most readable contemporary proponent, Hans Robert Jauss:

> the artistic character of a work [...] must in no way always be immediately perceptible within the horizon [of expectation] of its first appearance [...]. The distance between the actual first perception of a work and its virtual significance, or, put another way, the resistance that the new work poses to the expectations of its first audience, can be so great that it requires a long process of reception to gather in that which was unexpected and unusable within the first horizon. It can thereby happen that a virtual significance of the work remains long unrecognized until the 'literary evolution', through the actualization of a newer form, reaches the horizon that now for the first time allows one to find access to the understanding of the misunderstood older form. [...] One can line up the examples of how a new literary form can reopen access to forgotten literature. These include the so-called 'renaissances' – so-called, because the word's meaning gives rise to the appearance of an automatic return, and often prevents one from recognizing that literary tradition can not transmit itself alone. That is, a literary past can return only when a new reception draws it back into the present, whether an altered aesthetic attitude willfully reaches back to reappropriate the past, or an unexpected light falls back on forgotten literature from the new moment of literary evolution, allowing something to be found that one previously could not have sought in it.[10]

It is this 'altered aesthetic attitude' which I wish to pursue, specifically the aesthetics of the Enlightenment, which marks the reflowering of European interest in Dante.

Several of the words in my title cry out for elucidation. A start has been made on 'reception'. 'Enlightenment' must come next. Eric Hobsbawm has glossed some current views thus: 'These days the Enlightenment can be dismissed as anything from superficial and intellectually naive to a conspiracy of dead white men in periwigs to provide the intellectual foundation for Western imperialism'.[11] Such views derive ultimately from the Frankfurt School – Horkheimer, Adorno, and those of like mind. A long-term defender of the Enlightenment, Roy Porter, on the other hand, recognizes a methodological need for 'better mapping [...] of the contacts and circuits of the literati and their listeners. The loops between London, Edinburgh and Dublin, between the metropolis and the provinces, between cultures high and low, religious and secular, male and female'.[12] These loops – 'local knowledge' par excellence – are a useful way into the problem of Dante's pre-Romantic revival. And that problem concerns the paradox of why exactly an Age which prided itself on an ideal of reason and lucidity rather than fear and superstition, should turn to the revival of a text which had been neglected for centuries, a text moreover which takes the reader through the realms of the Dead, through terror and pity, to Catholic beatitude. On the face of it, Dante's text is an unlikely candidate for revival.

Writing the literary history of Italy at the turn of the eighteenth century, Arcadians of stature such as Ludovico Muratori and G. M. Crescimbeni were still dismissing the *Commedia* without having read it, or at least not having read it with insight and empathy, relying instead on received wisdom, or to be less kind and perhaps more accurate, on a prejudice bred of ignorance. This is not to say that the *Commedia* remained entirely unread for centuries. The history of new editions of Dante, however, indicates a distinct lack of popular demand, which may be attributed in part to Catholic censorship.[13]

This neglect began to change in the course of the eighteenth century, when even foreigners became acquainted with the text. We know that Thomas Gray, intoxicated by the sublime heights and depths of the Alps, translated the Ugolino episode in around 1739–40. But he seems to have regarded this as marginal activity, because the translations were never published in his life-time. But this is a straw in the wind. The seminal re-awakening comes in mid-century, with new Italian editions, with Giuseppe Baretti, and with a select band of enthusiasts, artists, and patrons – including Joshua Reynolds – based in Rome in the early 1750s. Reynolds' painting of Ugolino – now in a private collection – played a considerable role in the rise of a Gothic sensibility in Britain. But if we are searching for an alteration in the aesthetic attitude, we must look to a man who never set foot in Rome, or in Italy at all, but who was intimately acquainted with many of the select band of artists and patrons in 1750s Rome. And that man was Edmund Burke, whose *Philosophical Enquiry into our Ideas concerning the Beautiful and the Sublime* (1757, 2nd edition 1759) ushered in an 'altered aesthetic attitude'.

Without straying too far into biography it may be useful to sketch in some of Roy Porter's loops, which mesh together and help to account for Dante's rehabilitation in the British Isles, a rehabilitation which took hold well before the Romantics. There is one well-known and obvious connection between Baretti and Burke, and he is Samuel Johnson. Baretti somehow came under Johnson's wing on his arrival in London in the early 1750s. Burke had also arrived recently with his eye on a career in the law and in public life, but with his head also full of literary and philosophical ideas, and with a tortured religious sensibility. Johnson certainly came into contact with both of them. They may even have come into direct contact with each other. Even if they did not, there is very little doubt that Burke knew of the Ugolino episode – which inspired the Reynolds painting – and that it played at least some part in the development of what we might call 'the aesthetics of terror' which would shortly manifest itself in Burke's *Philosophical Enquiry* and in the new genre of Gothic fiction which would be ushered in, anonymously, by Horace Walpole in *The Castle of Otranto* (1765), a work which purported to be a translation from a little-read medieval Italian source. Something akin to Orientalism was going on, *avanti la lettera*, where southern, medieval, Catholic Italy, as the Other for northern, enlightened, Protestant Britain, was being explored as exotic, transgressive, and therefore seductive.

I have put matters thus, using the currency of Edward Said's concept almost as a modern cliché, presenting a piece of literary history in teleological terms, as if it were the inevitable outcome of an Enlightenment interest in Italy. Of course, there was nothing remotely inevitable about it. The interpretation, while it may be current and fashionable, does not actually explain *why* any of it should have happened, or else it explains away too much. For more focus, we need to dig deeper into the documented historical record, and restore the real hidden connection between Baretti, Reynolds, Burke, and Walpole, the revival of Dante, and the project to translate all of the *Commedia* into English for the very first time. And that connection does exist, like one of Roy Porter's loops.

The key protagonist is James Caulfeild (1728–99), fourth Viscount Charlemont and later first Earl of Charlemont. He and Burke had been friends in Dublin in the 1740s when Burke was an undergraduate. They maintained a regular epistolary friendship until they fell out over the French Revolution, shortly before Burke's death. Where Burke was relatively poor, Charlemont was phenomenally wealthy, leaving Dublin in 1746 – some years before Burke – on a Grand Tour of nine years' duration, a tour which brought him into direct contact with Baretti at the Accademia reale in Turin. Charlemont left Turin to go south, on to Greece, Turkey, and Egypt, before returning to Rome for nearly four years. Baretti, on the other hand, went north, through Paris to London, where he spent much of the rest of his life. As with Burke, Charlemont maintained contact until Baretti's death. At Rome, Charlemont set up a short-lived Academy of British Artists and was an early patron of various artists including Pompeo Batoni, Piranesi, and of course Joshua Reynolds. So, Baretti, Burke, and Reynolds were all corresponding with Charlemont, and kept apprised of each other's activities. There is a fourth piece of the jigsaw: Horace Walpole – who had accompanied Gray across the Alps in 1739 – was also among Charlemont's correspondents, and Charlemont possessed first editions of all Walpole's books, including the anonymous *Castle of Otranto.*

The British Enlightenment interest in Dante is symptomatic of a line which witnessed on the one hand literary frauds such as *The Castle of Otranto*, the *Ossian* poems, and on the other some early attempts at systematic literary history, e.g. Bishop Percy's *Reliquies of Ancient Poetry* (Percy, the Bishop of Dromore, was another of Charlemont's friends – the first edition of the *Reliquies* was published, like *The Castle of Otranto*, in 1765), Samuel Johnson's *Lives of the Poets*, and Thomas Warton's three-volume *History of English Poetry* (which includes a discussion of Dante). These were early attempts at professional literary history in English, but they have an important predecessor from earlier in the century. Voltaire, after all, had written his *Essay on Epic Poetry* (1727) in English. Dante does not figure in that work at all. A generation later, Dante had been rehabilitated in Voltaire's mind, mostly through the agency of Italian ex-patriates such as Paolo Rolli and Baretti, also writing in English, as it happens. The problem, for the English-reading public was that there was no complete translation of the text, and never had been. Without any doubt that is why Lord Charlemont agreed to provide financial support to Henry Boyd, a young Anglican priest in the west of Ireland, so that Boyd might make good this deficiency.

Boyd began working on his translation in the early 1780s. He seems not to have been discouraged by the fact that 1782 saw a complete translation of *Inferno* (by Charles Rogers) and a very partial one (the first three cantos, translated by William Hayley, later to be Blake's patron). Boyd's version of *Inferno* appeared, with notes and some two hundred pages of introductory matter, in 1785. It was promptly panned by an anonymous critic in the *Edinburgh Review*. Lord Charlemont also had grave concerns for his pet project, to the point where he began his own annotated translation. Boyd, however, was not to be deflected from his intentions and he produced his complete translation in 1802, well before Cary's complete version (1814), usually claimed, incorrectly, as the first complete English translation.

Did Boyd's Dante deserve to be panned? On a number of grounds, that may be the case. Firstly the reader may be surprised to see what has happened to Dante's *terza rima.* Where Cary would opt for Miltonic blank verse, Boyd chose the route of the six-line stanza. This is just one example of Boyd's 'improving' the text. Charlemont himself identified a related problem, and that concerned Boyd's sanitizing crude or vulgar passages from *Inferno.*[14] The third criticism is that Boyd makes significant departures from Dante's text. The precise nature of these departures remains to be charted in a subsequent project, but they are significant at least in number.

Where before critics may have been content to dismiss Boyd's version as 'quaint' and to dismiss the pre-Romantic interest in Dante as irrelevant, this can no longer remain the case. There has been significant new scholarship in the last decade which has brought to light (a) new sources such as the Charlemont translations, previously unknown, (b) new theoretical concerns, e.g. Translation Theory, Reception Theory, and (c) a revival of interest in pre-Romantic readings of Dante, represented by Nick Havely's edited book on *Dante's Modern Afterlife* and the William Blake exhibition in the Tate gallery in 2001. These developments run in parallel with significant advances in the digital technologies which now allow for the democratization of sources not readily available and tools for dealing more scientifically with such texts.[15] The digital technologies allow for the presentation of enormous chunks of text, e.g. all the eighteenth-century translations of Dante into English and French, cross-referenced to each other and to an original. This can also allow for sophisticated operations such as concordancing.[15]

It may be useful to cite one example of how these rediscovered sources and the new technologies can provide us with a thicker interpretation of Dante's 'naturalization' in eighteenth-century Britain. Running a co-occurrence search on Boyd's text, I came across four examplars of the collocation 'Arno's Vale'. This collocation does not translate anything specific in Dante's text. Therefore, given that it is not an isolated occurrence, it may be suspected that there is contamination from another source, that something is going on of which the translator is aware, but which we do not understand, though it may have had meaning for the original audience. 'Arno's Vale', in fact, was a popular song in mid-eighteenth-century Britain, but there is no particular reason why Boyd should have imported the title of a popular song into his translation. More significantly, it is the name of a stately house in Bristol, seat of the Hervey family, the Earls of Bristol. Francis Hervey, the Earl Bishop of Derry, was a flamboyant Grand Tourist, and bitter political and cultural rival of Lord Charlemont. I suspect – though there is further digging to be done – that Boyd broke with Charlemont early in his project, and allied himself with the Earl Bishop (which would have been a shrewder career move), dedicating his translation of *Inferno* (1785) – but not the complete work in 1802 – to Hervey. The otherwise incomprehensible import of the family seat into the translation is to be read as homage in those terms. Examples such as this begin to clarify some of the uses to which Dante was put, as do Boyd's notes, which make very clear indeed that he was being read – in the British Isles at least – through the filter of Burke's aesthetics. Thus a paradigm shift was in progress, and Dante's canonization as Poet of the Sublime was established well before the advent of the Romantics.

NOTES

1 P. Toynbee, *Dante in English Literature from Chaucer to Cary (c.1380–1844)* (London: Methuen, 1909).
2 R. C. Marshall, *Italy in English Literature 1755–1815* (New York: Columbia University Press, 1934).
3 W. P. Friedrich, *Dante's Fame Abroad, 1350–1850* (Chapel Hill, NC: University of North Carolina Press, 1950).
4 C. P. Brand, *Italian and the English Romantics: the Italianate Fashion in Early Nineteenth-century England* (Cambridge: Cambridge University Press, 1957).
5 See W. J. de Sua, *Dante into English* (Chapel Hill, NC: University of North Carolina Press, 1964), G. H. McWilliam, 'Some Notes on the Irish Contribution to the Pre-romantic Rediscovery of Italian Literature', in *Italian Presence in Ireland: A Contribution to Irish-Italian Relations*, edited [anonymously] for the Istituto italiano di cultura, Dublin (Dublin: Istituto italiano di cultura, 1965), 51–77, and G. F. Cunningham, *The Divine Comedy in English: A Critical Bibliography*, 2 vols (Edinburgh-London: Oliver & Boyd, 1965–66). See also B. Corrigan, *Italian Poets and English Critics, 1755–1859* (Chicago-London: University of Chicago Press, 1969). More generally, each of the following contribute to research in the field: A. Vallone, *Storia della critica dantesca dal xiv al xx secolo*, 2 vols (Padua: Vallardi, 1981); *Dante in America: The First Two Centuries*, ed. A. B. Giamatti (Binghamton, NY: Center for Medieval and Early Renaissance Studies, 1983); *Dante: The Critical Heritage 1314(?)–1870*, ed. M. Caesar (London-New York: Routledge, 1989); V. Tinkler-Villani, *Visions of Dante in English Poetry: Translations of the 'Commedia' from Jonathan Richardson to William Blake* (Amsterdam: Rodopi, 1989); M. Menocal, *Writing in Dante's Cult of Truth: From Borges to Boccaccio* (Durham, NC-London: Duke University Press, 1991); *L'opera di Dante nel mondo*, ed. E. Esposito (Ravenna: Longo, 1992); D. Wallace, 'Dante in English', in *The Cambridge Companion to Dante*, ed. R. Jacoff (Cambridge: Cambridge University Press, 1993), pp. 237–58, *Dante's Modern Afterlife*, ed. N. Havely (London-New York: Routledge & St Martin's Press, 1998); and *Lord Charlemont's History of Italian Poetry from Dante to Metastasio*, ed. G. Talbot, 3 vols (Lewiston, NY-Lampeter: Edwin Mellen Press, 2000).
6 R. Kirkpatrick, *English and Italian Literature from Dante to Shakespeare: a Study of Source, Analogue and Divergence* (London: Longman, 1995).
7 For various examples, see C. Geertz, *The Interpretation of Cultures: Selected Essays* (London: Hutchinson, 1975).
8 T. S. Eliot, 'Tradition and Individual Talent' (1919), now to be found in his *Selected Prose*, ed. J. Hayward (London: Penguin, 1953), pp. 21–30.
9 See W. Benjamin, 'The Task of the Translator', now to be found in H. Zohn's English translation in W. Benjamin, *Illuminations*, ed. H. Arendt (London: Fontana, 1973), pp. 61–82, and in various anthologies of texts fundamental to translation studies.
10 H. R. Jauss, *Towards an Aesthetic of Reception*, transl. T. Bahti (Brighton: Harvester, 1982), p. 35.
11 Hobsbawm is cited in R. Porter, *Enlightenment: Britain and the Making of the Modern World* (London: Allen Lane, 2000), p. 12.
12 Porter, p. 12.
13 The *Monarchia* remained on the Index until 1881.
14 This is an issue Edoardo Crisafulli has addressed recently in relation to Cary's version. See E.Crisafulli, 'Taboo Language in Translation', *Perspectives: Studies in Translatology*, 5, no. 2 (1997), 237–56. There is potential for an amusing parallel study here, taking in Boyd's translation, and indeed Charlemont's. For a freely available electronic version of Boyd's translation, see http://www.hull.ac.uk/dante.
15 Indeed a number of Dante websites have taken advantage of digital technologies to link up text and image. For Italian text, Cary and Longfellow translations, and illustrations from the famous Vellutello edition (1544), from Sandro Botticelli, from Gustave Doré, and from Salvator Dalì, see the excellent website at http://www.divinecomedy.org/divine_comedy.php3.

THE TAMING OF DOSTOEVSKY: A NOTE ON ENGLISH TRANSLATIONS OF *CRIME AND PUNISHMENT*

Patrick Corness
Coventry University

The present essay samples the treatment of some features of Russian discourse in various published translations into English of Dostoevsky's novel *Crime and Punishment*, seen from a cultural-historical perspective. It focuses on a perceived attenuation of stylistic effect in the translations, attempting, for reasons of space, merely to hint at the nature of the issue by touching on a selected aspect of this topic with reference to a few examples.

The best-known translations of Dostoevsky, as well as of many other major nineteenth-century Russian authors, are those by Constance Garnett (1862–1946), who may almost be said to have invented Russian literature for English readers; perhaps one should say re-invented, for her works are in some sense more like English novels than Russian novels in English – a levelled-out, highly respected canonical Russian literature in English.[1] Historically, a remarkable achievement, but from an objective cultural standpoint some shortcomings should also be noted. Carolyn Heilbrun has expressed the view that 'of all the criticisms made of Constance Garnett's translations, that which notices her tendency to neutralize the styles of the Russian writers is probably the most valid'.[2] Glyn Turton defended her version of Turgenev's *Rudin* against sterner critics, but admits her stylistic shortcomings in rendering peasant speech in this novel, in that she 'makes scarcely any distinction between the idiom in which the peasantry speak and that used by the gentry'.[3] Kornei Chukovsky remarked that the Garnett translations 'would have been considerably better if they had been submitted at the time of their publication to the intense scrutiny of critics [...]. But there was no criticism'.[4] Chukovsky went so far as to declare that, apart from her Turgenev, they were all 'insipid, pale and – worst of all – trivial'.[5] A. N. Nikoliukin found that in *The Brothers Karamazov* Garnett 'to a certain extent smoothed out the novelist's stylistic distinctiveness and "Russian way of thinking"', and he concluded that 'those English and American writers who spoke of Dostoevskii's influence on their own writings knew a rather different novelist from the one familiar to Russian readers'.[6] More recently, Peter France has commented, referring to analysis by Nikoliukin and others, that 'she shortens and simplifies, muting Dostoevsky's jarring contrasts, sacrificing his insistent rhythms and repetitions, toning down the Russian colouring, explaining and normalizing in all sorts of ways'.[7]

The novel was originally introduced to the English reader in 1886, five years after the death of Dostoevsky. This version, by Frederick Whishaw, is still in print today, albeit, scandalously, without acknowledgement of his work by the publisher.[8] Whishaw's translation was, to put it politely, incomplete; Simeon Rapoport supposed that he made omissions 'because, being himself a novelist, he held himself a better judge of what is of interest to the reader than Dostoevsky himself'.[9]

The early reception of Russian novels in English translation was governed by the prevailing taste in literature in late Victorian England. As Gilbert Phelps writes, 'the truth of the matter is that Dostoevsky's fictional methods were utterly incomprehensible to those accustomed to the traditional forms of nineteenth-century English fiction'.[10] Joseph Conrad, not the most russophile of commentators, remarked in 1912, in a letter to Constance Garnett's husband: 'Of course your wife's translation is wonderful. One almost breaks one's heart merely thinking of it. What courage! What perseverance! What talent of – interpretation, let us say. The word "translation" does not apply to your wife's achievements. But indeed the man's art does not deserve this good fortune. Turgenev (and perhaps Tolstoy) are the only two really worthy of her'.[11]

In an interview for the BBC shortly before her death, Garnett expressed her view that Dostoevsky was 'so obscure and so careless a writer that one can scarcely help clarifying him – sometimes it needs some penetration to see what he is trying to say'.[12] But the interruptions, repetitions, and other 'untidiness' are of course functional. Constant 'interruption' of the narrative by the author is a deliberate technique whereby he seeks to reinforce the 'truth' of the portrayed 'reality'. This is one reason why, as I. A. Zundelovich writes, the composition and linguistic structure are characterized by 'that convulsive, passionate tension which renders Dostoevsky's style inimitable'.[13]

Rachel May's *The Translator in the Text*, a critical analysis of traditional approaches to the translation into English of narrative discourse in the Russian novel, addresses problems of cultural transfer, offering what the publisher refers to as 'a new paradigm for translation criticism'.[14] Her illustrative excerpts provide a stimulus to further investigation, presenting in effect a number of hypotheses which deserve to be followed up by empirical investigation into extant translations. Kornei Chukovsky's criticism of Garnett's work is too far-reaching to discuss in a brief essay. The single excerpt from *Crime and Punishment* made by May will therefore be addressed, as her analysis prompts further comment, and brief additional examples from this novel will be considered in an attempt to illustrate the nature of the issues raised, focusing on the role of repetition in Dostoevsky's style.

May's example of the 'penetrative word' technique in Dostoevsky[15] (i.e. deliberate repetition to create an echo between narrator and fictional character) taken from Part 6, Chapter 5 of the novel, reveals the loss of this effect in translation, but the commentary introduces a further confusion regarding the compounding of this loss by a certain semantic inaccuracy, or at least ambiguity, in the Garnett version:

> Он стоял перед нею *в двух шагах*, ждал и смотрел на нее дикою решимостью, воспаленно-страстным, тяжелым взглядом. Дуня поняла, что он скорее умрет, чем отпустит ее. 'И... и уж, конечно, она убъет его теперь, *в двух шагах*!'
>
> Вдруг она от*бросила* револьвер.
> – *Бросила*! с удивлением проговорил Свидригайлов и глубоко перевел дух.

Garnett translates this as:

> He stood facing her, *two paces away*, waiting and gazing at her with wild determination, with feverishly passionate, stubborn, set eyes. Dounia saw that he would sooner die than let her go. 'And... now, of course she would kill him, *at two paces*!' Suddenly she *flung away* the revolver.
>
> 'She's *dropped it*!' said Svidrigailov with surprise, and he drew a deep breath.[16]

There are two cases of repetition here (identified by my italics). As May points out, most of the translations do not retain 'these internal echoes'. Garnett, she says, 'repeats "two paces", but entirely elides the other repetition'.[17] In fact, the echo effect is more than a little diminished by the translator's variation of the phrase in the first case ('two paces away', 'at two paces'), while in the second ('she flung away the revolver', 'She's dropped it!') the damage done is greater than May suggests, because of the apparent misinterpretation of the second verb. In the original, the effect of the echo from the repetition is enhanced by the word-play on the objective meaning of the first verb 'отбросила': 'she threw it aside' (narrator) and the metaphoric meaning of the echoing, un-prefixed verb 'бросила': 'She's given up' (Svidrigailov). Garnett's 'She's dropped it' seems not to be meant in this sense.

Other versions are semantically more accurate than Garnett's but make no attempt to render the echo: 'Suddenly she flung down the revolver. / "She has given up" '. (Jessie Coulson); 'Suddenly she flung the revolver aside. / "She's given up the idea!" '(David McDuff), while Richard Pevear and Larissa Volokhonsky unequivocally revert to the presumed error by Garnett: 'Suddenly she threw the revolver aside. / "She threw it down!" '[18] David Magarshack's version is nearest to achieving an echo effect, but he also, though less unambiguously, perpetuates the misinterpretation of the second verb, 'бросила': 'Suddenly she threw away the gun. / "Thrown it away!" '[19] Sidney Monas's (American) version is similar: 'All of a sudden she threw away the revolver. / Svidrigailov said in surprise, "She threw it away!"'[20] May's own suggestion offers no improvement on Monas. She finds a way of rendering an echo, but seems to reject Coulson and McDuff's reading, which I share, of the metaphoric significance of '*бросила*': 'Suddenly she *threw* the revolver *away* from her. / "*Threw* it *away*!", muttered Svidrigailov in amazement, taking a deep breath' (my italics).[21] An echo could perhaps be achieved as follows, at the expense of a certain loss of dramatic gesture in my rendering of the first verb: 'Suddenly she dropped the gun. / "She's dropped the idea." '

An even more striking example of Garnett's attenuated, restrained Dostoevsky in *Crime and Punishment* is her treatment of the style, and indeed the content, of Raskolnikov's emotional inner monologue in Part 1, Chapter 4. His torment as he learns of his sister's sacrifices on his behalf is calmed by Garnett, who tones down the vocabulary, elides emotionally reinforcing repetitions, and makes other omissions, abridging and distorting the content and couching it in less expressive language which dilutes the emotional impact:

> Жертву-то, жертву-то обе вы измерили ли вполне? Так ли? Под силу ли? В пользу ли? Разумно ли? Знаете ли вы, Дунечка, что Сонечкин жребий ничем не сквернее жребия с господином Лужиным?

> Have you taken the measure of your sacrifice, both of you? Is it right? Can you bear it? Is it any use? Is there sense in it? And let me tell you, Dounia, Sonia's life is no worse than life with Mr. Luzhin.

The emphasis and focus given by the repetition of 'жертву', 'sacrifice', the key semantic concept in this paragraph, yet further reinforced by the enclitic '-то', a device for drawing attention to a topic, are missing in this translation. Only Coulson, and Pevear and Volokhonsky (the latter generally the most literal interpreters), at least repeat the word 'sacrifice' here. Magarshack, instead of repeating the word 'sacrifice', adopts the (stylistically, in English) effective strategy of repeating the question about awareness of it: 'Is either of you aware of the sacrifice you've made? Have you measured it fully?' He also effectively renders the '-то': '*the* sacrifice *you've made*' (my italics).

Raskolnikov's series of imploring rhetorical questions, repeating the stylistically marked, emphatic interrogative particle 'ли', builds a certain emotional crescendo which is lacking in the varied, stylistically unmarked, un-emphasized interrogatives in Garnett's translation. She replaces one of the interrogatives by a weak imperative: 'And let me tell you', introducing additional stylistic variety which further dilutes the impact. Magarshack gives emphasis to just two of the six questions by adding 'are you quite sure?': 'But are you *quite sure* you have the strength to go through with it?'; 'Are you *quite sure* it is worth it?' (my italics). Coulson renders emphasis in a similar way, but applies it to different questions: 'Will it *really* bring *such* great benefits?' and 'Is it *really* sensible and wise?' (my italics).

Thus some translators render Dostoevsky's emphasis, variously and selectively, but none attempts to do so systematically; the insistent, emphatic repetitiveness is at least partially lost. Magarshack's strategy of repetition with variation is perhaps dictated by the demands of English received stylistics, tenets which are at odds with Dostoevsky's reinforcingly repetitive style. Magarshack seeks to render focus and emphasis in certain cases by a more discursive strategy, whereas other translators, by following the original fairly closely, render more faithfully the somewhat staccato effect of the original. However, neither strategy renders the overall style and tone evoked by the particles '-то' and 'ли', which have no literal equivalents in English.

Garnett's 'life' is a semantically and emotionally weak translation of 'жребий', 'fate', and the same applies to 'worse', which is substituted for a more expressive and more pejorative epithet referring to that fate: 'сквернее', literally 'nastier', 'fouler', 'more vile'.[22] All the other translators have 'fate', except Pevear and Volokhonsky, who have 'lot' (etymologically exact). Coulson and Pevear and Volokhonsky are satisfied with a 'worse fate', against Whishaw's and Magarshack's 'degrading (fate)' and McDuff's 'uglier (fate)'.

There are some omissions by Garnett. The original speaks of *fully* taking the measure ('вполне'), but she disregards this adverb and omits a further reinforcing device from the final sentence: '*ничем* не скverнее', '*by no means* any nastier' (my italics). Other translators include both of these features. In a literal sense, Pevear and Volokhonsky are the most accurate translators and they most consistently fill in gaps in earlier versions.

Actual errors are not unknown in otherwise good translations, and as a post-script to this example it should be noted that Raskolnikov's elliptical third question has been mis-read by one translator. McDuff quite erroneously renders 'Под силу ли?'('Can you cope with it?'; 'Have you the strength for this?') as 'Is it being made *under duress*?' (my italics). This is a case of simple non-recognition of the idiomatic phraseme 'под силу'.

In my next example, from the same passage in Part 1 Chapter 4, the question 'понимаете?' 'do you understand?' occurs four times, again with the emphatic interrogative particle 'ли': '*Понимаеше ли, понимаеше ли, понимаеше ли* вы, что значит сия чистота? *Понимаеше ли* вы, что лужинская чистота все равно что и Сонечкина чистота' (my italics). The impact of the repetition, reinforced by the emphatic particle 'ли', might be rendered as: 'Do you understand, ... *do* you? ... do you *really* understand what this purity means? Are you sure you understand?' This effect is attenuated in all the translations studied; considerations of English style seem to have dictated the reduction of the first three occurrences to two; in the case of the earlier versions by Whishaw and Garnett to only one: 'But do you understand what this cleanness means? Do you understand?' (Whishaw);[23] 'Do you understand what that smartness means? Do you understand?' (Garnett); 'Do you realize, do you realize what this "cleanliness" means? Do you realize?' (Magarshack); 'Do you understand, do you understand, what that cleanness means? Do you understand?' (Coulson); 'Do you realize, do you realize what that kind of cleanliness involves? Do you realize?' (McDuff); 'Do you understand, do you understand what this cleanliness means? Do you understand?' (Pevear and Volokhonsky).

The treatment of the hyphenated repetition of an adverb may be considered in the following example, taken from the conclusion of the letter from Raskolnikov's mother in Part 1 Chapter 3 which prompts the ensuing internal monologue discussed above: ' Обнимаю тебя *крепко-крепко* и целую бессчетно' (my italics). The double hyphenated adverb 'крепко-крепко' is semantically equivalent to the simplex adverb 'крепко', 'firmly', preceded by the intensifier 'очень', 'very'. Stylistically, this is a device with a strong, emotive impact. It may be either colloquial-informal, as here, or literary-poetic. The example might therefore be rendered as 'I hug you ever so tightly and send lots of kisses' or 'A big, big hug and lots of kisses'.

Garnett, notwithstanding her tendency elsewhere to eliminate repetition, translates it, rather awkwardly, perhaps, as: 'I embrace you warmly, warmly, with many kisses', not rendering effectively the emotionally expressive hyphenated adverb pair in Russian. Other translators offer a variety of pragmatic solutions: 'I embrace you a thousand times and with kisses without end' (Whishaw); 'Let me hold you close to me, my darling, and kiss you again and again' (Magarshack); 'I send you all my love, and many, many kisses' (Coulson); 'I hug you tight as tight, and send you kisses without number' (McDuff); 'I embrace you very, very warmly, and send you countless kisses' (Pevear and Volokhonsky).

In the case of the brief excerpts considered above, the respective translations render semantic components with varying degrees of success or completeness, whereas there seems to be a persistent reluctance to render repetitiveness and a difficulty in rendering aspects of tone and style governed by those elusive devices which apparently have no semantic content but which lend a particular pragmatic and stylistic colour to the text as a whole. The question as to how typical this is of English translations of Dostoevsky and whether such features of Russian style can be rendered more closely in English calls for a more in-depth study.

Notes

1 She translated some seventy volumes of the works of Turgenev, Gogol, Dostoevsky, Tolstoy, Chekhov, Ostrovsky, Goncharov, Gorky, and others. A complete list is given by R. Garnett, *Constance Garnett: A Heroic Life* (London: Sinclair-Stevenson, 1991), pp. 36–62.

2 C. G. Heilbrun, *The Garnett Family* (London: George Allen & Unwin, 1961), p. 193.

3 G. Turton, 'Turgenev in the Context of English Literature, 1850–1900', University of Warwick PhD thesis, 1984, p. 307.

4 K. Chukovsky, *The Art of Translation: Kornei Chukovsky's 'A High Art'*, transl. and ed. L. Leighton (Knoxville: University of Tennessee Press, 1984), p. 222.

5 Chukovsky, *The Art of Translation*, p. 222.

6 A. N. Nikoliukin, 'Dostoevskii in Constance Garnett's Translation', transl. W. J. Leatherbarrow, in ed. W. J. Leatherbarrow, *Dostoevskii and Britain* (Oxford-Providence: Berg, 1995), p. 226.

7 P. France, 'Dostoevsky', *The Oxford Guide to Literature in English Translation*, ed. P. France (Oxford: Oxford University Press, 2000), p. 595. The references are unspecified.

8 This all too common phenomenon of cultural blindness in the English-speaking world is discussed as 'the translator's invisibility' by L. Venuti, *The Translator's Invisibility: A History of Translation* (London-New York: Routledge, 1995).

9 S. Rapoport, 'Translations and Translators: Mainly from the Russian', *Contemporary Review*, 133 (1928), 504.

10 G. Phelps, *The Russian Novel in English Fiction* (London: Hutchinson, 1956), p. 3.

11 H. Muchnic, 'Dostoevsky's English Reputation (1881–1936)', *Smith College Studies in Modern Languages*, 20 (1938–39), pp. 3–4.

12 C. Garnett, 'Russian Literature in English', *The Listener*, 30 January, 1947, p. 195.

13 Я. О. Зунделович, 'О стиле романа Ф М Достоевского Преступление и наказание', *Труды Узбекского университета*, вып. 72 (1957), с. 118 (my translation).

14 R. May, *The Translator in the Text: On Reading Russian Literature in English* (Evanston: Northwestern University Press, 1994).
15 The term was used by Mikhail Bakhtin, e.g. in his *Problems of Dostoevsky's Poetics*, transl. and ed. C. Emerson (Minneapolis-London: University of Minnesota Press, 1984), p. 255.
16 F. Dostoevsky, *Crime and Punishment*, transl. C. Garnett (New York: Macmillan, 1914).
17 See May, *The Translator in the Text*, p. 113.
18 For the various English translations, see F. Dostoevsky, *Crime and Punishment*, transl. J. Coulson (Oxford-New York: Oxford University Press, 1953); F. Dostoevsky, *Crime and Punishment*, transl. with an introduction and notes by D. McDuff (London: Penguin, 1991), F. Dostoevsky, *Crime and Punishment*, transl. and annotated R. Pevear and L. Volokhonsky (London: Vintage, 1993).
19 F. Dostoevsky, *Crime and Punishment,* transl. with an introduction by D. Magarshack (London: Penguin Books, 1951). May seems to suggest that Magarshack himself has thrown away his opportunity to achieve the desired effect here, remarking: 'but he unaccountably alters the tense' (*The Translator in the Text*, p. 113). Of course, 'has thrown' could not be replaced by a repeated 'threw' here, except in American English, where the subtle distinction between perfect tense and past simple hardly exists.
20 F. Dostoevsky, *Crime and Punishment*, transl. S. Monas (New York: Signet, 1968), as quoted by May (the Monas translation was not available to me).
21 *The Translator in the Text*, p. 113
22 Colloquially, 'скверный' denotes merely 'bad', but the general tone of the context implies the stronger meaning. Predictably, perhaps, Garnett is among the translators choosing the 'weaker' option.
23 F. Dostoevsky, *Crime and Punishment* (Philadelphia-London: Courage Books, 1996). Text reprinted from the first English-language translation [by Frederick Whishaw], published in 1886 by Vizetelly, London.

ON TRANSLATING POETRY

Alessandro Gentili
James Madison University, Florence

In the last ten years or so, many conferences, special editions of literary reviews, and books have been dedicated to the craft, or even art, of translating poetry. All this *mondan romore* has certainly lent dignity to the translator's trade, for too long, in my opinion, after my years of translating twentieth-century Irish poetry from English into Italian, looked down on as a minor craft subordinate to the art of writing. Far too much, however, has been written and theorized about translation, which is more often than not an exercise *against* method. Each translation is a single and unique act of incongruence, often sheer folly. It is a single and unique act for it proves impossible to define objectively what may determine the spirit and the nature of each individual poetic translation. According to the discipline called *traduttologia* in Italian, the essential question is whether a translation is source- or target-oriented? In other words, is a translation to allow the target-language reader to grasp the sense of the parent text, or to appreciate the new text in the light of his or her own parent language and culture? The affirmation itself presents a dilemma, but either process is enigmatic, for translation is also synonymous with interpretation. We cannot, for instance, translate Dante without coming first of all to interpretative decisions about the *Commedia*. To a wide range of variables in the parent text (metrics, versification techniques, different forms of aesthetics, styles, etc.), there corresponds a wider range, indeed a labyrinth of attitudes and possible solutions, all of them conceivable in the mind of the translator. The fact remains that translating poetry is an obscure encounter of two opposites: the text to be translated in its seemingly uneasy position of acquiescence, and the process of translating that seems to have the privilege, the advantage, or disadvantage, of proposing and disposing.

Just two samples of poetical translation make my position clear: a fragment from Mario Luzi's version of *The Rime of the Ancient Mariner* and Robert Lowell's imitation of Montale's *L'anguilla* (*The Eel*). Translating poetry is a desperate attempt at reduplicating that which cannot be reduplicated. Poetry is unseizable, intangible. Poetry depends on the word, and immediately transcends the word. Poetry can only be lovingly contemplated. Yet, we keep on translating and the outcome is something completely different from the original. One starts from home, from the 'foul rag and bone shop of the heart', from one's own vision of things. Mario Luzi's elegant hendecasyllables from his *Ballata del vecchio marinaio* give expression to a landscape and a state of mind which recall his own lines 'La terra senza dolcezza d'alberi, la terra arida/che rompe sotto Siena il suo mareggiare morto'.[1]

L' aria profonda esplose di vivezza! Cento vessilli in fiamme luminosi guizzavano su e giù, di qua, di là, e gli astri vi danzavano nel mezzo.	The upper air burst into life! And a hundred fire-flags sheen, to and fro they were hurried about! and to and fro, and in and out, the wan stars danced between.
Il vento emise un sibilo più forte, stormivano le vele come biada; e la pioggia crosciava giù dal nembo oscuro che la luna bianca orlava.	And the coming wind did roar more loud, and the sails did sigh like sedge; and the rain poured down from one black cloud; the Moon was at its edge.
La densa e nera nuvola fu rotta ed ancora la luna era al suo fianco: come acque cadenti d'alta roccia il fulmine sfrecciò giù senza un guizzo, tale un fiume spazioso cade a picco.	The thick black cloud was cleft, and still the Moon was at its side: like waters shot from some high crag, the lightning fell with never a jag, a river steep and wide.[2]

The hill-land of Siena, indeed 'su e giù, di qua, di là' and rolling with 'biada', is Luzi's vision of the ocean, of the enigma: 'inganno o verità,/ miraggio o evidenza'.[3] On the other hand, translating Coleridge, a poet of narrative rather than analogical imagination, helped Luzi in his long process of loosening the tense and dense knots of his own lyrical symbolism, a process that lasted nearly twenty years, from *Primizie del deserto* (1952) to *Nel magma* (1963). In Luzi's own words: 'In Coleridge trovavo proprio quello che forse andavo cercando, cioè quei toni intermedi che in fondo erano stati compressi nella lirica anteriore, che era andata per simboli molto addensati. Sentivo invece il bisogno di articolare il discorso in modo da fruire anche di queste possibilità di sfumatura, di *nuance* che ha una lingua'.[4] For the Italian translation, his model is Dante. Luzi's collection of essays *L'inferno e il limbo* (1949) was the theoretical starting point for a rediscovery of Dante's multiplicity of styles, which constitute the spirit of the *Commedia*. The exercise of translating from Coleridge turned out to be a workshop which served Luzi's purpose of reworking his poetical language according to the archetype of Dante's narrative and diction: 'cento *vessilli* in fiamme luminosi' ('divenisser signaculo in *vessillo*', *Par.* XXVII, 50); '*guizzavano* su e giù, di qua, di là' ('ché i Pesci *guizzan* su per l'orizzonta', *Inf.* XI, 113, cf. *Inf.* V, 43 'di *qua*, di *là*, di *giù*, di *sú*, li mena'; 'per che sì forte *guizzavan* le giunte', *Inf.* XIX, 26; '*guizza* dentro a lo specchio vostra image', *Purg.* XXV, 26); 'e la pioggia *crosciava* giù dal nembo' ('che cotai colpi per vendetta *croscia*', *Inf.* XXIV, 120); 'come acque cadenti *d'alta roccia*' ('cadea *de l'alta roccia* un liquor chiaro', *Purg.* XXII, 137). Is this then Coleridge translated, Dante revisited, or Luzi experimenting with a new aesthetics? It is precisely the act of incongruence which puzzles the reader.

For his own imitation *The Eel*, Lowell draws from his Atlantic verse repertoire.

The Eel

The eel, the North Sea siren,
who leaves dead-pan Icelandic gods
and the Baltic for our Mediterranean,
our estuaries, our rivers –
who lances through their profound places,
and flinty portages, from branch to branch,
twig to twig, thinning down now,
ever snaking inward, worming
for the granite's heartland, threading
delicate capillaries of slime –
and in the Romagna one morning
the blaze of the chestnut blossoms
ignites its smudge in the dead water
pooled from chisellings of the Apennines...
the eel, a whipstock, a Roman candle,
love's arrow on earth, which only
reaches the paradise of fecundity
through our gullies and fiery, charred streams;
a green spirit, potent only
where desolation and arson burn;
a spark that says everything
begins where everything is clinker;
this buried rainbow, this iris, twin sister
of the one you set in your eye's target centre
to shine on the sons of men,
on us, up to our gills in your life-giving mud –
can you call her *Sister*?[5]

L'anguilla, la siren
dei mari freddi che lascia il Baltico
per giungere ai nostri mari,
ai nostri estuarî, ai fiumi
che risale in profondo, sotto la piena avversa,
di ramo in ramo e poi
di capello in capello, assottigliati,
sempre più addentro, sempre più nel cuore
del macigno, filtrando
tra gorielli di melma finché un giorno
una luce scoccata dai castagni
ne accende il guizzo in pozze d'acquamorta,
nei fossi che declinano
dai balzi d'Appennino alla Romagna;
l'anguilla, torcia, frusta,
freccia d'Amore in terra
che solo i nostri botri o i disseccati
ruscelli pirenaici riconducono
a paradisi di fecondazione;
l'anima verde che cerca
vita là dove solo
morde l'arsura e la desolazione,
la scintilla che dice
tutto comincia quando tutto pare
incarbonirsi, bronco seppellito;
l'iride breve, gemella
di quella che incastonano i tuoi cigli
e fai brillare intatta in mezzo ai figli
dell'uomo, immersi nel tuo fango,
puoi tu non crederla sorella?

Geographical and mythical terms, such as 'North Sea' and 'deadpan Icelandic gods', while revealing Lowell's passion for exactitude as well as for meaningful resonances, are reminiscent of poems such as 'The North Sea Undertaker's Complaint',[6] 'Mother Marie Therese',[7] and of the powerful elegy 'The Quaker Graveyard in Nantucket'.[8] By contrast, or to keep a balance against 'the Baltic', Lowell feels the need to make clear that Montale's 'nostri mari' are actually 'our Mediterranean', which is indeed 'nostrum mare'. The description of the eel's movement follows Montale's text. However, verbs and images such as 'thinning down now,/ever snaking inward, worming/for the granite's heartland', particularize still further Montale's particularities, intensify and heighten the stages of the eel's upstream darting to the source, making them more solidly visible and palpable. The measured and controlled nature of Montale's original bursts out ('a Roman candle') in the sanguine temperament of Lowell's 'siren [...] threading/[...] capillaries of slime'. When the long journey of the eel comes to an end, which is also a new beginning, the exposure to the light is then exalted by the entry of 'Romagna'; in this context the placename sounds particularly open and luminous. Finally, the question 'can you call her *Sister*?', the Franciscan word 'sister' ('sorella') in italics, reads more loving and at the same time more directly dramatic than the cautious original 'puoi tu/non crederla sorella?' We are here confronted with two distinct poems. Lowell writes in the introduction to his *Imitations*:

> This book is partly self-sufficient and separate from its sources, and should be read as a sequence, one voice running through many personalities, contrasts and repetitions. [...] I have tried to write live English and to do what my authors might have done if they were writing their poems now and in America. [...] I believe that poetic translation – I would call it an imitation – must be expert and inspired, and needs at least as much technique, luck and rightness of hand as an original poem.[9]

In June 1961 T. S. Eliot had written to Lowell on the question of Lowell's translation project:

> I think that the right title for this is *Imitations* [...]. I think also that a subtitle is a mistake: your translations are indeed imitations, and if you use the word translation in the subtitle you will attract all those meticulous little critics who delight in finding what seem to them mis-translations [...]. Keep the word translation out of it.[10]

Faithfulness in translating poetry is a myth. However, like Lowell following the suggestion of T. S. Eliot, we might well return to Leopardi's idea of *imitazione*:

> E certo ogni bellezza principale nelle arti e nello scrivere deriva dalla natura e

> non dall'affettazione o ricerca. Ora il traduttore necessariamente affetta, cioè si sforza di esprimere il carattere e lo stile altrui, e ripetere il detto di un altro alla maniera e gusto del medesimo. Quindi osservate quanto sia difficile una buona traduzione in genere di bella letteratura, opera che dev'esser composta di proprietà che paiono discordanti e incompatibili e contraddittorie. E similmente l'anima e lo spirito e l'ingegno del traduttore. Massime quando il principale o uno de' principali pregi dell'originale consiste appunto nell'inaffettato, naturale e spontaneo, laddove il traduttore per sua natura non può essere spontaneo. Ma d'altra parte quest'affettazione che ho detto è così necessaria al traduttore, che, quando i pregi dello stile non sieno il forte dell'originale, la traduzione inaffettata in quello che ho detto, si può chiamare un dimezzamento del testo, e quando essi pregi formino il principale interesse dell'opera (come in buona parte degli antichi classici) la traduzione non è traduzione, ma come un'imitazione sofistica, una compilazione, un capo morto, o se non altro un'opera nuova.[11]

Poetry is evasive, as evasive as Daphne to Apollo who in pursuit of her eventually finds himself embracing a wrinkled trunk. Poetry is *forma formans*, that can only 'contain' itself. A translation is instead an attempt at having an original text 'contained' in some new content; which is an absurdity, or at least a reversal of what poetry is. Yet we keep on translating; for incongruence, absurdity, even folly itself, are tempting, intriguing, and at times enlightening. Translating poetry can only find its reason for existence in an absorbing, obsessive passion for a text, a language, or an aesthetics, as well as in a desire to participate closely in, and to have an affinity with, a poet's life. It is an act which subjects our reason to desire.

To such desire I, too, have subjected my reason. After reading and rereading a text to find and possess a poem's being in its form, in order to make the contents mine, to absorb them, I set out on my journey of translation, trying to ferry that text to my side of the river. After a first draft in pencil, I move slowly toward a second draft, which I then cast aside to let the dregs settle only to return to it when the signs seem right. Another metaphor I, as a fisherman, can use, is that of fly-fishing: a discipline of patience, exact casting, and timing, until you hook a trout that has to be landed in live. I keep thinking and working gently away on the second draft, still in pencil, glad to have something to work on, coming back to it in a colder form and tinkering with it until I reach the stage where I type it up, most recently on a floppy disk. Going through the process of typing up, a form of scanning almost, I look at my work again and see whether it can be improved. At that stage, friends join in and help. Usually, Gaetano Prampolini of Florence University, Fabrizio Dall'Aglio, *redacteur extraordinaire* of Passigli Editori, and the poet Mario Luzi, editor of the Passigli Editori poetry series, all cast a warm eye on my translation work. Pleasant meetings and discussions always follow – the act of incongruence turned into a friendly game of skill – till the typescripts are collected and the welcome suggestions eventually find their place in the final draft, as they did in the following:

Windharp	*Arpa eolia*
for Patrick Collins	*a Patrick Collins*
The sounds of Ireland, That restless whispering You never get away From, seeping out of Low bushes and grass, Heatherbells and fern, Wrinkling bog pools, Scraping tree branches, Light hunting cloud, Sound hounding sight, A hand ceaselessly Combing and stroking The landscape, till The valley gleams Like the pile upon A mountain pony's coat.[12]	Suoni d'Irlanda, Incessante sussurrare A seguire… Fruscia da cespi, Ciuffi d'erba, Erica, felci, Crespe torbiere, Ispide frasche, Luce bracca nubi, Suono segugio alla vista, Mano che senza posa Pettina e liscia Il paesaggio, Finché la valle fulge Come manto Di pony di montagna.[13]

John Montague's *Windharp* is the kind of poem a passionate and tenacious translator, indeed extravagant more than earnest, takes as a true challenge: 'un invito alla lepre a correre'. The text itself can work as a short score which a piano player may interpret and play according to his own sense and ear. The sounds, not the semantics, are to be re-created here; and the sounds of a country can only be carefully listened to, absorbed, and reproduced by an interpreter right there where they originally seep out. As a matter of fact, my *Suoni d'Irlanda* found their first form on a breezy day in the countryside around my second family home in Co. Kerry. They were finally revised, placed, and pondered in Tuscany. The images 'Luce bracca nubi,/Suono segugio alla vista' were suggested to me by Mario Luzi.

The enriching encounter between two linguistic and cultural media, which the true act of translating creates, gives us the perspective and an experience of living within two dimensions of reality and reference. We see our own language and literary tradition from the outside, from a distanced position which enables us to focus more sensibly. We see the foreign language and culture from within, with the eye of close reading. This, together with that absorbing, obsessive passion for a poetics, is what may justify the act of incongruence.

NOTES

1 'La terra senza dolcezza d'alberi, la terra arida', in M. Luzi, *L'opera poetica* (Milan: Mondadori, 1998), p. 487.

2 S. T. Coleridge, *La ballata del vecchio marinaio*, transl. M. Luzi (Milan: Biblioteca Universale Rizzoli, 1973), pp. 104–05.
3 Luzi, p. 487.
4 M. Luzi, M. Specchio, *Luzi, leggere e scrivere* (Florence: M. Nardi Editore, 1993), pp. 53–54.
5 R. Lowell, *Imitations* (London: Faber and Faber, 1962), pp. 125–26.
6 R. Lowell, *Poems 1938 –1949* (London: Faber and Faber, 1970), p. 43.
7 Lowell, *Poems*, pp. 87–90.
8 Lowell, *Poems*, pp. 18–22
9 Lowell, *Imitations*, pp. xi–xii.
10 T. S. Eliot to Robert Lowell, 1 June 1961 (Houghton Library).
11 G. Leopardi, *Zibaldone di pensieri,* 319–20 (Milan: Mondadori, 1983), p. 217.
12 J. Montague, *A Slow Dance* (Dublin: The Dolmen Press, 1975), p. 28.
13 A. Gentili, *Rosa di macchia, Antologia della poesia irlandese dopo Yeats* (Florence: Passigli Editori, 1992), p. 161, and J. Montague, *Arpa eolia*, transl. A. Gentili, with an engraving by S. Ferrari (Reggio Emilia: Mavida Edizioni, 1996).

CARPE TECNOLOGIA

Brian McCarthy
University of Wollongong

Beautiful dust-free chalk on squeak-proof blackboards does not cause students to learn well. Neither do high-powered computers. What counts is what teachers can cause to happen in the minds of their students by the agency of a given piece of technology or combination of technologies. This contribution is not a broad survey of recent work in the field of CALL, and it is inductive rather than deductive in approach. It examines the shared pedagogical and practical characteristics of two CALL software development projects in an attempt to identify features which have contributed to the success and longevity of what might in many respects be considered quite dissimilar pieces of work. The first is the project for Advanced Technical Translation (*TransIt-TIGER*) emanating from the University of Hull, the second a suite of materials to support beginner and intermediate foreign-language French studies at the University of Wollongong in Australia. Although eventually reaching much wider publics, both projects were initially focused on the needs of a very restricted group of learners, and neither is particularly sophisticated on the technical level. Impetus for development in each case derived largely from the desire on the part of an individual academic to continue to teach effectively in a constantly changing university environment and from a recognition of the computer's potential to enhance delivery, and hence students' chances to achieve, in specific learning tasks. Both benefited from restricted but real opportunities and resources to explore; from the impetus of early small successes; and from the support of colleagues through either expertise in programming and software design, or a genuine interest in the outcomes.

The purpose is not to reiterate earlier full accounts of the materials, so their introduction here will be limited to broad outlines. Further details of the *TransIt-TIGER* activity, and a sense of its evolution in relation to the broader educational environment of the day, can be found in the literature.[1] Linguistic, pedagogical, and practical facets of the development of the Wollongong materials have been the subject of numerous articles.[2]

TransIt is essentially a framework for a three-phase computer-focused approach to translation as a class activity:

(a) the students' first translation is on-screen, in a class situation, with electronic access to technical glossaries, dictionaries, a thesaurus, and hints drawing attention to ticklish points which students will need to address;
(b) a preliminary shorthand correction by the teacher of a hard-copy version of the first translation indicates the appropriateness of solutions proposed by the student;
(c) a final translation is produced by students once they have had an opportunity to analyse further their first translation using the teacher's flagging of problem areas in conjunction with two stylistically different, externally-generated translations of the same passage.

The Wollongong project produced two technology-based innovations, one for grammar, the other for basic speaking skills. For grammar review and maintenance, a comprehensive set of computer-based activities was developed between 1990 and 2000. These activities are textbook-independent; their purpose is to:

(a) draw questions randomly from large banks of items;
(b) offer on-line grammar assistance, animated help screens, and built-in error analysis feedback;
(c) incorporate audio support where appropriate;
(d) present easily-digested, carefully sequenced work units; and
(e) allow the teacher to monitor student performance.

At Wollongong, students are required to achieve a prescribed score in designated revision units using the open-access computer laboratory prior to sitting for the scheduled class test on that unit. Both the preparation and the class test are compulsory elements of the course, and are repeated in each semester of enrolment in the French major.

The basic speaking skills activity ('En tête-à-tête') combines a lecture-room exercise whose efficacy is not affected by class size (students have paired-speaking cue cards) with audio-supported computer back-up. The print materials consist of 300 pairs of cards, each containing: (a) a cue or series of cues in English which the speaker is required to communicate to his/her partner at the appropriate point in the dialogue; (b) the text of what the speaker is most likely to hear from his/her interlocutor at each stage of the dialogue.

The software backup in the computer laboratory contains text and audio versions of all 300 dialogues. For each item the computer displays the cues in sequence. Students click to hear any line of dialogue (and variants where applicable), and can choose to view or conceal the corresponding lines of text. They may also choose to play the full dialogue.

The Hull and Wollongong materials, on the surface, have little in common. They were developed in different institutional contexts and for students working with different languages. One is for advanced students coming to grips with technical translation, the other for near-beginners mastering basic grammar and oral communication skills. In terms of design principles and inspiration, however, they are constructed on remarkably similar frameworks. Both projects were needs-based. Foreign-language learning is a curious mix of academic reflection and skills acquisition, requiring guidance, explanation, carefully structured activities, and a great deal of practice. Two significant obstacles are the foreignness of the learning context, and the traditional patterns of university instruction. Essentially, 'foreign' means that when students leave the classroom they enter a world that provides little or no opportunity for fruitful encounters with the language they are studying. Over the calendar year, for every hour in class, students spend something like forty or fifty in a foreign-language wilderness.

Partly for resource reasons, but also because of the type of academic guidance required, humanities subjects traditionally provide students with three hours of teaching a week over approximately half of the calendar year, and frequently in large classes. This is decidedly unconducive to foreign-language learning, and even less so to foreign-language acquisition. In an environment where institutional pressures are in the direction of increasing class sizes, reducing contact hours, and limiting choice, teachers are constantly on the look-out for ways to improve the use of class time merely to retain the status quo in terms of quality and standards. As an instrument for managing information, both in terms of quantity and delivery patterns, the computer has enormous potential. But it remains potential until somebody actually locates or generates the information, and conceives and constructs ways of causing students to interact with it, and to emerge from that interaction with new understanding.

Both projects were realistic in that they had restricted, clearly-defined objectives. It is easy for administrators or the technically-assured to have visions of large unsupervised laboratories crammed for eighteen hours a day with full-fee paying foreign-language students who emerge at the end of a ten-week course equipped to perform as interpreters for high-level trade delegations on sensitive missions to a range of European and Asian countries. It is also easy, particularly after the sobering lessons of the language-laboratory era, for academics to recoil from any idea of entrusting any aspect of teaching or learning to machines. The Hull and Wollongong projects were neither fantastically grandiose nor technologically-timorous. Each took as its starting point a specific, routine problem associated with one facet of language learning, with a manageable group of students in a familiar institution. The line followed was that: 'No one will be able to claim to be an expert in the field of technical translation, even after completing this course. Nevertheless, all will…'.[3] It was a case of small scope, clear focus, and willingness to build and refine. One of the factors contributing to the eventual success of the projects, but largely unrecognized at the outset, was that the design teams included typical, experienced, competent language teachers. This meant not only that they were addressing problems faced by a large group of colleagues, but that the solutions they produced had instant wider application. They may not have invented a foreign-language learning panacea, but an undisputed advance, however restricted, has to be worth more than a shattered dream.

When institutional directors or bureaucrats conduct time and motion studies, they are invariably budget driven. Academics, on the other hand, are inclined to be interested in economy of effort for simpler, more primitive reasons: it leaves time to pursue different goals, scholarly or otherwise. Software development is a notorious consumer of time and energy, and the stimulus it provides for the designer-developer is likely to be short-lived if the product has a limited shelf life in a single corner store. One way of economizing effort is to produce materials that are text-book independent and not subject to the fashions and vagaries of teaching methodologies. This makes the material transportable in time – a good technique is a good technique, and it can be plugged into any number of teaching environments. Both sets of material under consideration here have respected that principle.

The attractiveness of a piece of software is also greatly enhanced if it economizes other people's effort, if the message conveyed to colleagues is 'I've done the work, we can all take advantage of it', rather than 'I've done the work, the results are good, now you too can do the work, and your results will also be good'. Not a particularly attractive offer if 'the work' is measured in hundreds or even thousands of hours.

In the case of the *TransIt* material, the vicarious work is in the construction of an authoring shell, a technically refined and pedagogically run-in template allowing others to use the existing material or to build from the existing base to create new materials for existing or additional languages. In the case of the Wollongong materials, the spade-work for the grammar activities included the creation of reservoirs containing so many items that students could return to an activity as many times as they desired or needed to without ever duplicating an exercise, and the structuring of modules in such a way as to allow students either to focus on discrete aspects of the grammar point or to undertake a comprehensive review. For the 'En-tête-à-tête' speaking activities, the items are speech acts likely to be of use in everyday communication. Collectively they represent a distillation of the notions, structures, functions, situations, grammar, register, and vocabulary found in a range of contemporary textbooks and manuals.

While very concerned to account for their pedagogical and linguistic foundations, neither project presumes to establish rules to govern use of the materials in other contexts. They provide a resource, they do not impose a methodology. Thus, for *TransIt*, for example, the class dynamic, the relationship between the written work and computer work, the status and extent of the teacher's grading of the translations, and the nature and range of the on-line assistance employed are all flexible and a function of the institutional environment.

To label teaching materials as 'student-centred' can create misconceptions. It implies that the teacher is peripheral. The most learner-centred educational situation could thus be considered to be that of enrolling students in a subject and leaving the rest up to them. Clearly, neither of the projects is student-centred in that sense. Yet in both of them the teacher is physically peripheral compared, for example, to the situation in a typical lecture. This physical absence is only possible because the teacher's influence has been injected into the software. Creating a learning environment that will allow students to achieve specified learning objectives independently requires considerably more thought and preparation than a lesson in a conventional classroom where the teacher is always present as information source and operations manager. The teacher's presence in a piece of software is similar to the parental presence inherent in safe toys. In addition to identifying, evaluating, organizing, presenting, and commenting on materials, the physically absent teacher must anticipate the full range of difficulties likely to be encountered by individual students with different backgrounds and learning styles, and take pre-emptive action by designing software that organizes and presents information accordingly. The spirit of the teacher is in fact doubly present in student-centred CALL materials.

Another shared characteristic of the Hull and Wollongong software is miscibility. In neither case did the authors view the electronic materials as holy, set apart from other media. For *TransIt*, the fact that a dictionary is on line does not make the use of other printed or human references taboo, and the preliminary corrections are made on hard copy of the text. The computers have been used only for what they are good at, and the scope of that use, like the content and design of the materials they manage, is in the hands of the teacher. The mingling of media to meet learner needs in the face of new institutional constraints is well illustrated by the case of 'En tête-à-tête'. At Wollongong, in response to pressure for foreign-language subjects, including beginner classes, to operate under the same staff-student ratio and class-size formulae as other humanities subjects, there were essentially two choices: keep small classes and reduce the number of class hours, or keep the number of face-to-face hours for students, but in a single large class. For beginner students, six hours per week over the twenty-six weeks of the academic year already gives them the unenviable task of mastering the basics of a foreign language in 156 hours. The large-class option was considered preferable to that of reduced face-to-face contact, so the methodology had to change. Classes to date have contained between thirty-five and sixty students. In each class a small number of cued dialogue sequences is presented by the teacher on overhead transparencies (students are already familiar with the vocabulary, speech functions, and grammar, as a result of other classwork); each student is given a set of cue cards and works through the dialogues with a partner; they repeat the activity, reversing roles; the computer-based text and audio support is available for revision in an open-access laboratory.

Methodologically it is a compromise, but the approach succeeds in generating a lot of student-monitored, worthwhile, intelligible, simulated communication between students in the lecture theatre, and a lot of questions either between students or from students to the lecturer. It also alerts students to any areas of weakness in their skills. And come assessment time, staff can be confident that students were fully resourced to accomplish the task set, and students failing to master these speaking skills are aware that the problem did not lie in a lack of opportunity or resources.

Both projects were built on a desire to optimize students' use of time. They had the benefit of sustained exposure to collegial critique; they developed robustness from constant trial and modification in the light of feedback from users; both were very important learning processes for the designers; and both were fully integrated into language courses.

Because a decade has now elapsed since their inception, it is perhaps appropriate to conclude by stepping back a pace and looking at some of the ways in which the educational backdrop to CALL, and hence the currency of software such as that produced at Hull and Wollongong, has changed with time.

In 1991 it made sense for teachers requiring students to use computers as an integral part of their course to be concerned that this component might be greeted with apprehension, scepticism, or hostility, or even by a blank refusal to learn. Sensitivity to such attitudinal obstacles had no doubt been developed in part through the teachers' own reactions in encountering various facets of the new medium for the first time. In the intervening time, the staggering inroads made by computers into so many areas of daily activity have almost totally eliminated the once very real concern that the medium itself might prove an obstacle to learning. That shift was to be expected.

At the same time a second, somewhat subtler shift has occurred in many institutions – a climate change with the potential to act as a retardant to the growth of CALL materials precisely at the time when they are most needed. In the early 1990s, when CALL was new, and teachers and administrators alike were only vaguely aware of its potential, it was possible to embark on a software development project with a certain ingenuous enthusiasm. It represented a stimulating challenge, and nobody quite knew where it might lead. Material circumstances and institutional policy placed little obligation on the teacher-developer in terms of shaping the output. It was an era of exploration. Ten years down the track, when universities' corporate images are increasingly being built on their capacity to demonstrate innovative and productive use of information technology, and ever-shrinking budgets accentuate the need for cost efficiency and income generation, and devolve responsibility for them down the chain, the position of the CALL-curious lecturer has undergone a sea change.

Traditionally, the creativity of academics, including the type that manifested itself in the production of the CALL materials we have focused on here, has been the product of a free but strongly self-disciplined spirit with an urge to discover and impart knowledge. Many university foreign-language teachers now embarking on software development will be required to do so with an awareness that their creativity is sanctioned only insofar as it can be harnessed by their employer, and that their output is viewed from the outside as an educational commodity. Such a shift has probably been inevitable. But it has the potential to strait-jacket academic initiative and to cause resentment, discouragement, or demotivation. It is difficult, and a little unsettling, to imagine what its full impact might be on the future of CALL development.

NOTES

1 See D. Thompson and J. Thompson, 'Advanced (Technical) Translation (Italian/English): A Pilot Project', in *Language Learning with Computers, An Educational Challenge*, ed. P. Baumgartner and A. Hall (Klagenfurt: WISL, 1991), pp. 160–73; D. Thompson and J. Thompson, *TransIt, Advanced [Technical] Translation (Italian to English) Teacher's Manual* (Hull: Department of Italian, University of Hull, 1993), and J. Thompson, 'Embedding Technology into Language Examinations: A Case Study', in *Active Learning*, 4 (1996), 25–29.

2 See B. N. McCarthy, 'Discerning the Teacher behind the Software', *ReCall*, 6, no. 2 (1994), 23–28; B. N. McCarthy, 'Designing Materials for Computer Assisted Language Learning: Some Preliminary Considerations', *BABEL – Journal of the Australian Federation of Modern Language Teachers' Associations*, 29, no. 3 (1994), 24–27 and 36; B. N. McCarthy, 'Grammar Drills: What CALL Can and Cannot Do', *ON-CALL – The Australian Journal of Computers and Language Education*, 9, no. 2 (1995), 30–41; B. N. McCarthy, 'Fully Integrated CALL: Mission Accomplished', *ON-CALL – The Australian Journal of Computers and Language Education*, 10, no. 2 (1996), 15–28; B. N. McCarthy, 'Needs-Driven French Materials Development: Practicalities and Theories', *Carnet Austral, Bulletin of the Australian Society for French Studies*, 11 (1999), 9–18; B. N. McCarthy, 'It Needn't be CALL-or-nothing: A Case of Computers as Partners not Managers in a Multimedia Teaching Kit', *CALL-EJ Online*, 2, no. 2 (2001) (http://www.clec.ritsumei.ac.jp/english/callejonline/5-2/contents2-2.html)

3 D. and J. Thompson, 'Advanced (Technical) Translation (Italian/English)', p. 1.

TRANSLATION AND TECHNOLOGY: AN OVERVIEW OF THE ADVANCED COMPUTER TOOLS AVAILABLE TO THE TRANSLATOR

Federica Scarpa
University of Trieste

As compared to even the recent past, a major role in the competence of today's translator is played by her ability to use the computer tools available on the market to help improve productivity and the quality of output. Nowadays we take for granted the translator's ability to use the resources provided by word-processing (including the applications for desktop publishing and 'proofing tools' such as spelling/grammar checkers and thesauri) as well as on-line terminology databases/off-line electronic dictionaries such as *Eurodicautom* (europa.eu.int/eurodicautom) and the innumerable CD-ROMs available on the market. However, beyond this, and especially in non-literary translation, there is the opportunity of using 'advanced' software tools which can be integrated in workstations specifically aimed at translators ('integrated translation systems' or 'translator workstations'). The advanced tools that will be dealt with in this contribution are the translator-specific resources for automatic and computer-assisted translation and the more general linguistic tools provided by terminology management systems.

A great deal of translation work consists of the application of tedious and repetitive tasks that the translator should be able to mechanize in order to focus on solving the real translation problems and thus provide her clients with a higher-quality service. The software tools providing the translator with ready-made translations based on previously translated material fall into the two main categories of fully automatic translation (or machine translation, MT) and machine-assisted translation (MAT, or computer-assisted translation, CAT). MT and MAT tools can be further subdivided into human-aided machine translation (HAMT) systems, where the automatic element is predominant over the human one, and machine-aided human translation (MAHT) systems, where the predominant element is conversely the translator.

Within the broad category of research and tools known as Universal Translator/Interpreter,[1] MT is 'limited' to the automatic translation of written text from one language to another. The basis of most MT systems is provided by abstract linguistic representations which are used in all the three phases of the process: (1) parsing (or analysis), where a parser works bottom-up analyzing the source sentence, assigning each word to grammatical categories and grouping words into bigger components – some structural, others semantic – organized in tree-structures; (2) transfer, where comparative grammar rules adapt the source-language structures to target-language constructs (*I like that film/Mi piace quel film*) and each source-language word is replaced with its target-language correspondent; (3) synthesis, where a synthesizer works top-down from the representation of the target sentence to a full translation via syntactic and morphological generation.

Variations on this three-stage model include the work being carried out by the Natural Language Laboratory of the School of Computing Science at Simon Fraser University (British Columbia) on a method known as 'partial parsing', which analyzes chunks of language rather than breaking down the structure of entire sentences to try to minimize syntactically ambiguous translations, and the two-stage model skipping the transfer stage – the weakest link in the chain – and based on 'interlinguas', i.e. sentence representations which are totally language independent.

Broadly speaking, MT systems can be knowledge-based, example-based, or statistical. Knowledge-based translation systems, modelled on Artificial Intelligence, refer to an encyclopaedic knowledge of the world and a knowledge of words and their combinations. This type of knowledge imitates the structuring of world experience in the human mind and consists of the creation of a network of connections and relations to form a complex hierarchy of concepts. The final product of knowledge-based systems such as *KANT* (knowledge-based accurate translation), which is being developed for technical documents at the Language Technologies Institute (LTI) of the Carnegie Mellon University in Pittsburgh, is a translation which aims at providing the meaning of the message, i.e. by paraphrasing a text rather than translating it. On the other hand example-based systems like *Diplomat*, another product being developed at LTI, are based on the possibility of accessing huge volumes of data and information both in the source and the target languages. As translation often consists in recalling or finding chunks of text which are similar to those to be translated, the basic idea underlying this type of MT system is that it is sufficient for the machine to draw the appropriate examples and their translation from previously translated texts which are stored as bilingual concordances. A mixed example- and knowledge-based approach is being developed at the Information Sciences Institute of the University of Southern California: the *ReWrite* project aims to create a system which can compare original and translated texts, then use that knowledge to teach itself to understand the new language using only original texts. Finally, statistical systems such as the software toolkit *Egypt* – which is being developed by a multi-university team led by Kevin Knight of the University of Southern California's Information Sciences Institute – use statistical methods to classify automatically the relationships among linguistic data in bilingual texts and apply those patterns to their translation functions. Statistical systems are usually incorporated in linguistic systems, where statistics is used to select or disambiguate a lexical item on the basis of its higher usage percentage, or in parsing and transfer stages in order to avoid the use of linguistic analysis.

On-line MT tools such as *Systran*, powering the *Babel Fish* (babelfish.altavista.com) and *Voila* translators (tr.voila.fr), and *FreeTranslation.com* (www.freetranslation.com) provide far from readily-usable translations but can nevertheless be used for 'raw' translations, i.e. for understanding quickly the content of a web-based text or of an e-mail message, thus enabling the user to decide whether to have the text translated or post-edited by a human translator.

Completely automatic translation is however only one of the many options available to translators: in HAMT the human translator participates in what is primarily a computerized translation process to help the software before, during, and after the process. During pre-editing, the source text is 'treated' in order to adapt the vocabulary and the structures of the text to the capabilities of the machine and to minimize the problems encountered during the translation process. In interactive systems human intervention is required during the translation process to carry out tasks such as clarifying an ambiguity in the source text and choosing among alternative translations in the target text. During post-editing, the output of the MT is revised by a human translator either interactively, with the machine drawing the translator's attention to potential errors, or off-line, with the translator revising the target text in much the same way as in human translation.[2]

On the other hand, in MAHT it is the translator who makes all the necessary choices. The heart and soul of MAHT, Translation Memory, consists of one or more databases of ready-made sentence pairs which are automatically recalled whenever a source sentence in the new text to be translated finds a match which is either exact (100% match) or similar (fuzzy match). In the case of partial matches, the target sentence may be edited to match exactly the source sentence, and both source and target sentences may be added to the database. In the case of new source sentences, the translator may translate and also add these to the Translation Memory database, thus enabling the database to grow and increasing the chances of exact and near matches in future tasks. Previously translated material can be searched at the sentence and sub-sentence levels thanks to bilingual concordance systems, which align sentence pairs of the parallel source- and target-language texts.[3]

A program which is a hybrid between HAMT and MAHT is *TransType*, developed by the Laboratory for Applied Research in Computational Linguistics of the University of Montreal: after the human translator has begun typing a translation, this software takes over by drawing on its own databases to complete words and sentences.

In non-literary translation, up to 50% of the time required by the entire translation process is taken up by the search for the correct terminology;[4] an important part of the competence of the translator therefore consists in her ability to find reference material quickly and efficiently. Computer systems for the development and management of multilingual terminology databases enable the translator to build and update her own personal glossaries, thus ensuring both greater speed in delivery and terminological consistency. Whether the translator uses traditional dictionaries or electronic terminological tools, once she has found a translation correspondence the need arises to store such data efficiently in order to be able to find them quickly and apply them to a new translation situation. Such a process was once done manually but today can be carried out by computer programs which enable the translator first to search for a particular term without exiting the document and then to transfer such terms into the text straight from the terminology database. Through a feature which is known as 'active terminology recognition', known terms can be stored in the database, automatically highlighted by the program at their next occurrence in the text, and pasted into the word processor.

Moreover the use of these software systems for automatically building, searching, and managing terminology provides the translator with termbases which can be reviewed, corrected, and updated in a quick and precise way. Such termbases not only contain the terms of one or more specific fields in the source language and their translation in the target language, but also contribute extremely valuable additional information (definition, context of use, bibliographical source, etc.) which in traditional paper glossaries was limited by lack of space. In particular, the type of information to be included in a typical terminological record should include management, linguistic, conceptual, and bibliographical data for each language.[5] Management data consist of information on the dates a term was inserted in the database and was last updated, and on the author of the record. Linguistic data consist of information on spelling (variants such as *shelf life* and *shelf-life* or *sterilisation* and *sterilization*), grammar (part of speech, gender, number, e.g. *information* is always used in the singular), register (*computerized axial tomography* and *scan*), standardization, synonyms (*data protection* and *protection of personal data*), and graphical variants (*operating system* and *OS, match* and *computer match*). Conceptual data consist of the definition of the concept designated by the term, the context in which the term occurs, explanations and restrictions on the use of the term within the specific conceptual field being considered, and the conceptual relations of the term with other terms (subordination, antonymy, hyponymy, etc.). Lastly, bibliographical data consist of the references used for the terminological search (specialized manuals and journals, dictionaries, glossaries, experts in the field, etc.).

An example of a terminology management system is the software *Trados Multiterm*, which allows users to customize the structure of terminological records to their specific needs. Because of its flexibility, this tool has been used to create *TERMit* (Terminology for interpreters and translators), a terminology database which is being developed at the SSLMIT, University of Trieste, and is freely accessible on line.[6] *TERMit*, which currently consists of approximately 25,000 terms in Italian, English, French, German, Spanish, Russian, and Dutch, is specifically aimed at translators/interpreters and is a concept-oriented and multidirectional termbase, where correspondences are created on a conceptual basis. Thus the starting point for each record is a concept and not a given term: this means that a record contains all the terms that describe the concept and that the database can be searched in any language direction.

A particularly complex example of a *TERMit* record is provided at the end of this paper, where the concept designated in Italian by the term *autorizzazione all'immissione in commercio*, taken from the specialized field of Good Manufacturing Practice in the pharmaceutical industry, is provided in three different records for Italian (the reference language for which terminological equivalences are provided), English, and French.[7] Each record consists of one or more terms in a given language and various fields:

(a) system fields (relating to management data), which are automatically filled in when each new record is created (date of creation of the record, author of the record, etc.);

(b) conceptual fields are of two types: (1) the fields Subject, Subfield, and Concept are based on the Dewey Decimal Classification (Dewey 1993; 1996) and assign the concept to a specialist discipline (*Pharmacy*), a more specific subfield of such a discipline (*Good Manufacturing Practice*) and an even more specific subcategory (*manufacture*); (2) the fields Definition, Context, Note, Related words, and Types of relation contain respectively one or more definitions of the (main) term, one or more contexts, additional explanatory notes, the terms designating concepts which are in a direct conceptual relation with the concept corresponding to the main term, and the type of conceptual relation existing between the main term and the terms related to it (subordinate, superordinate, coordinate, antonym, and general);

(c) the linguistic fields contain grammatical and spelling information (Morphosyntax, Grammar, Category, Variant of), pragmatic information concerning use (Usage label: main term, common etc.; Regional label: Britain, United States, etc.) and register (Style label: formal, colloquial, official, etc.), semantic/lexical information where synonyms are discussed – suggestions are made about their degree of synonymy (Synonyms and Synonymy) and the term's inclusion in specialist dictionaries (Lexica), and collocational information dealing with the most frequent collocations containing the main term (Phraseology);

(d) the bibliographic field Source contains information about the references of the term, its definition and context – and the explanatory notes;

(e) the fields Equivalence it-en (or, depending on the languages, it-fr, it-de, etc.) contain information on the degree of equivalence between the two terms which, in the two languages, represent a given concept.

In today's professional translation, the quality of a translated text must be a compromise between adequacy of use, cost, and speed of delivery. As any professional translator worth her salt must know, the integrated use of machine- and machine-assisted translation and terminology management systems offers various benefits in terms of productivity, accuracy, and consistency. These tools prove to be particularly useful in very repetitive texts such as those to be found in localization where, especially in the case of updates of previous versions of the same product, the percentage of sentences which are repeated, either exactly or partially, is very high both in the documentation and the software. By eliminating the repetitive work, these tools allow the translator to concentrate on the more interesting aspects of her work, and generally improve productivity by between 30% and 50%.[8] Moreover, maintaining appropriate terminology and sentence databases for each individual client means achieving higher accuracy and consistency – and therefore better quality – in the product supplied.

Owing to the integrated use of these advanced tools, the traditional competence of the translator to create a text in a different language is increasingly evolving into an ability to intervene in the control and revision processes of the final translation product.

NOTES

1 A real-time Universal Translator/Interpreter would be a product that converts free-ranging speech into text, translates the text, and then recites it to a listener who does not understand the original language. The research areas involved in the production of such a tool are speech processing (to convert speech into text), machine translation, speech synthesis (to convert text into speech), speech translation (to convert speech from one language into speech of another), and natural-language processing (NLP), a field which stands on its own but contributes to the other four in order to understand the grammatical and semantic relations among words. For example, speech-to-speech translation systems which can be applied to situations where the lexicon is relatively restricted (e.g. travel planning) have been developed between Swedish and English by the joint efforts of the Californian SRI and Swedish telecom, and between English and Japanese by the partnership of AT&T Labs in New Jersey with the Spoken Language Processing Group of the Advanced Telecommunications Research in Kyoto.

2 H. L. Somers, 'A Practical Approach to Using Machine Translation Software', *The Translator*, 3, no. 2 (1997), 193–212 (195–96).

3 In particular, when using previously translated material to build a translation memory, Uwe Reinke remarks on the usefulness of the alignment of the available parallel corpus at the sub-sentential level to improve the performance of translation memories, and he consequently advocates the incorporation of term-extraction software into translator workstations. See U. Reinke, 'Towards a Closer Integration of Termbases, Translation Memories, and Parallel Corpora – A Translation-oriented View', *TKE '99. Terminology and Knowledge Engineering, Proceedings of the 5th International Congress on Terminology and Knowledge Engineering* (Vienna: TermNet, 1999), pp. 527–43.

4 J. C. Sager, *Language Engineering and Translation Consequences of Automation* (Amsterdam-Philadelphia: John Benjamins, 1994), p. 206.

5 M. T. Musacchio, 'La terminologia orientata alla traduzione: aspetti teorici e problemi qualitativi', *Terminologia e traduzione assistita, Proceedings of the Seminar organized by AITI Sezione Veneto Trentino-Alto Adige and the Accademia Europea in Bozen* (Bolzano/Bozen, 31 October–7 November 1998, and Treviso, 26–27 February 1999), eds A. Furlanetto and R. Martini, CD-ROM of the special Supplement of the 'Bollettino regionale AITI Sezione Veneto Trentino-Alto Adige', 2 (1999).

6 See www.sslmit.units.it/termit/The features of *TERMit* have been described in much greater detail than here by M. Magris, 'Costituzione di una banca dati terminologica presso la SSLMIT di Trieste', *Rivista Internazionale di Tecnica della Traduzione,* 2 (1996), 138–51, and M. T. Musacchio, 'Terminology and Specialized Translation', *Textus*, Special issue on 'Translation Studies Revisited', ed. S. Bassnett, R. M. Bollettieri Bosinelli, and M. Ulrych, 12, no. 2 (1999), 369–89.

7 L. Giorgetta, *Le norme di buona fabbricazione dei medicinali: un'indagine terminografica in italiano,*

inglese e francese, unpublished degree dissertation, Scuola Superiore di Lingue Moderne per Interpreti e Traduttori, Università degli Studi di Trieste, Trieste (1997–98), pp. 56–60.

8 B. Esselink, *A Practical Guide to Software Localization* (Amsterdam-Philadelphia: John Benjamins, 1998), p. 135.

APPENDIX

Instance of Terminological Record in TERMit (Italian, English and French)

ITALIAN

Subject Pharmacy/Farmacia
Subfield Good manufacturing practice/Norme di buona fabbricazione

1) *it* **autorizzazione all'immissione in commercio** *Morphosyntax* noun group, f. *Usage label* main term
Source D.L.vo 178/91: art. 8
Definition Documento con valore legale rilasciato dall'Autorità competente e avente per oggetto la concessione dell'autorizzazione alla vendita di un medicinale. In esso sono riportati la composizione e la formulazione del medicinale per il quale l'autorizzazione è stata richiesta, le specifiche relative ai componenti e al prodotto finale (secondo quanto stabilito nella farmacopea in vigore o da altre fonti riconosciute), unitamente a particolari relativi alla confezione, all'etichettatura ed al periodo di validità del medicinale stesso.
Source Giorgetta 1998, cfr. WHO 1994: 12
Context Per le specialità medicinali contenenti componenti noti ma non ancora associati ai fini terapeutici, il richiedente l'autorizzazione all'immissione in commercio deve fornire i risultati delle prove farmacologiche, tossicologiche e cliniche relative all'associazione, ma non è tenuto a fornire la documentazione relativa a ciascuno dei singoli componenti.
Source D.L.vo 178/91: art. 8
Concept field fabbricazione
Related words autorizzazione alla produzione *Type of relation* coord.
Related words medicinale, specialità medicinale, domanda di autorizzazione all'immissione in commercio, richiedente l'autorizzazione all'immissione in commercio, detentore dell'autorizzazione all'immissione in commercio, dossier di autorizzazione all'immissione in commercio, fabbricante *Type of relation* general
Synonyms Benché 'autorizzazione alla commercializzazione' sia concettualmente un sinonimo di 'autorizzazione all'immissione in commercio', quest'ultimo è il termine ufficiale cui si fa riferimento nella legislazione italiana in materia (si vedano ad esempio i decreti legislativi D.L.vo 178/91 e D.L.vo 44/97). Il termine 'autorizzazione alla commercializzazione' si trova talvolta in testi più divulgativi. La sigla 'AIC' è piuttosto comune.
Equivalence it-en Equivalenza assoluta nell'ambito dell'Unione Europea. Corrispondenza funzionale con documenti dello stesso genere al di fuori dell'UE. Per quanto riguarda gli Stati Uniti, si hanno diversi tipi di 'autorizzazione'. L'iter e la terminologia cambiano a seconda del prodotto per il quale si richiede la registrazione. Ad esempio, la 'New Drug Application' è richiesta per i medicinali per uso umano, mentre per i medicinali biologici è necessaria la 'product license (application)'.
Equivalence it-fr Equivalenza assoluta nell'ambito dell'Unione Europea. Corrispondenza funzionale con documenti dello stesso genere al di fuori dell'UE.

2) *it* **AIC** *Morphosyntax* f. *Category* initials *Usage label* common
Source Battaglino 1996b: 20
Variant of autorizzazione all'immissione in commercio
Context I dettagli relativi alle aree di produzione, ad esempio le specifiche per la qualità microbiologica e l'assenza di particelle nell'aria, ricadono, normalmente, nel campo di applicazione delle NBF e non necessitano di essere descritte nella documentazione allegata alla domanda di

AIC, salvo richiesta specifica delle competenti Autorità.
Source Battaglino 1996b: 20

3) *it* **autorizzazione alla commercializzazione** *Morphosyntax* noun group, f. *Usage label* uncommon *Origin* loan translation
Source NBF CEE 1994: 40

ENGLISH
Subject Pharmacy/Farmacia
Subfield Good manufacturing practice/Norme di buona fabbricazione

1) *en* **marketing authorisation** *Morphosyntax* noun group *Usage label* main term *Regional label* Britain
Source Battaglino 1995: 30
Definition Legal document, issued by the competent drug regulatory authority, that establishes the detailed composition and formulation of the product, the pharmacopoeial or other recognized specifications of its ingredients and of the final product; and includes details of packaging, labelling and shelf-life.
Source WHO 1994: 12
Context The inspection should seek to verify, by means of examination of all relevant facilities, equipment and documents, that the information provided in the marketing authorisation application is being strictly adhered to.
Source Battaglino 1995: 30
Concept field manufacture
Related words manufacturing authorisation *Type of relation* coord.
Related words medicinal product, proprietary medicinal product, application for a marketing authorisation, applicant for a marketing authorisation, holder of a marketing authorisation, marketing authorisation dossier, manufacturer *Type of relation* general
Synonyms A purist approach to spelling rules suggests that the <-z-> variant should be adopted in this case. The American and purist British English spelling variant 'authorization' seems to prevail in EU documents, although the <-s-> variant ('authorisation') is found in more recent EU texts, following the prevailing British English spelling standards. The term 'market authorisation' was found only once, whereas the initials 'MA' are found in some unofficial texts. 'Product licence' and 'registration certificate' are only partial synonyms, in that these terms apply to countries outside the European Union. Indeed, although the concept behind the words is basically the same, some requirements may obviously be different. The term 'product licence' is defined in WHO 1994: 12 as 'An official document issued by the competent drug regulatory authority for the purpose of marketing or free distribution of a product. It must set out, inter alia, the name of the product, the pharmaceutical dosage form, the quantitative formula (including excipients) per dose (using international nonproprietary names or national generic names where they exist), the shelf-life and storage conditions and packaging characteristics. It also contains information approved for medical professionals and the public, the sales category, the name and address of the licence holder, and the period of validity of the licence'. 'Product licence' is the term which is used in the proposed guidelines on the WHO Certification Scheme (cf. WHO 1994: 12). The situation is rather different in the US: indeed, two terms are used as regards FDA approval of a product for marketing. For human use drug products, the term is 'New Drug Application' (or 'Abbreviated New Drug Application' for selected products), whereas the term 'Product License Application' (or 'product license') is used only for biological drug products for human use.

2) *en* **marketing authorization** *Morphosyntax* noun group *Category* spelling variant
Source Directive 91/356/EEC: art. 5
Variant of marketing authorisation
Context When a modification to the marketing authorization dossier is necessary, the application for modification must be submitted to the competent authorities.

Source Directive 91/356/EEC: art. 5

3) *en* **market authorisation** *Morphosyntax* noun group *Category* short form *Regional label* Britain
Source PLR 1997
Variant of marketing authorisation
Context As the market authorisation procedures cover both human and veterinary medicines, the situation relating to veterinary medicinal products is mentioned from time to time where there are significant differences.
Source PLR 1997

4) *en* **MA** *Morphosyntax* noun *Category* initials *Usage label* uncommon
Source Le Hir 1996: 230
Variant of marketing authorization

5) *en* **product licence** *Morphosyntax* noun group
Source WHO 1994: 12 *Synonymy* (~)

6) *en* **Product License Application** *Morphosyntax* noun group *Usage label* common *Regional label* USA
Source FDA 1997 *Synonymy* (<)

7) *en* **PDA** *Morphosyntax* noun *Category* initials *Usage label* common *Regional label* USA
Source FDA 1997
Variant of Product License Application

8) *en* **New Drug Application** *Morphosyntax* noun group *Usage label* common *Regional label* USA
Synonymy (<)
Phraseologisms Investigational New Drug Application
Source Skelly et al. 1993b: 162
Context A critical component is one which is formulated within the quantitative range given below, is specified in the New Drug Application (NDA/ANDA), and does not affect the release rate of drug from the dosage form.
Source Skelly et al. 1993b: 162

9) *en* **NDA** *Morphosyntax* noun *Category* initials *Usage label* common
Source Skelly et al. 1993a: 42
Variant of New Drug Application
Context All stability requirements for NDA's and ANDA's apply.
Source Skelly et al. 1993a: 42

10) *en* **Abbreviated New Drug Application** *Morphosyntax* noun group *Usage label* common *Regional label* USA *Synonymy* (<)
Source FDA 1997

11) *en* **ANDA** *Morphosyntax noun Category* initials *Usage label* common
Source Skelly et al. 1993a: 42
Variant of Abbreviated New Drug Application

12) *en* **Abbreviated NDA** *Morphosyntax* noun group *Category* short form *Usage label* uncommon
Source Gonzáles 1993: 92
Variant of Abbreviated New Drug Application
Context We will use this forum as a conduct to relay guidances of broad interest or changes in procedures which can influence the review processes for a New Drug Application (NDA) or Abbreviated NDA (ANDA).
Source Gonzáles 1993: 92

13) *en* **registration certificate** *Morphosyntax* noun group
Source WHO 1994: 12 *Synonymy* (~)

FRENCH
Subject Pharmacy/Farmacia
Subfield Good manufacturing practice/Norme di buona fabbricazione

1) *fr* **autorisation de mise sur le marché** *Morphosyntax* noun group, f. *Usage label* main term
Source Directive 75/319/CEE: art.11
Definition Document à valeur légale, accordé par les Autorités compétentes, décrivant en détail la composition et la formulation du produit, les spécifications de ses constituants et celles du produit final (selon les prescriptions de la Pharmacopée en vigueur ou d'autres sources reconnues), le conditionnement, l'étiquetage et la durée de validité du produit même.
Source Giorgetta 1998, cf. WHO 1994: 12
Context Il en est de même lorsqu'un ou plusieurs Etats membres ont suspendu ou retiré une autorisation de mise sur le marché, alors qu'un ou plusieurs Etats membres n'ont pas procédé à cette suspension ou à ce retrait.
Source Directive 75/319/CEE: art.11
Concept field fabrication
Related words autorisation de fabrication *Type of relation* coord.
Related words médicament, spécialité pharmaceutique, demande d'autorisation de mise sur le marché, demandeur d'autorisation de mise sur le marché, titulaire de l'autorisation de mise sur le marché, dossier d'autorisation de mise sur le marché, fabricant *Type of relation* general

2) *fr* **AMM** *Morphosyntax* f. *Category* initials *Usage label* common
Source Le Hir 1997: 1
Variant of autorisation de mise sur le marché
Context Les procédures de fabrication ont été, en principe, rédigées pour éviter toute dérive par rapport aux exigences des dossiers d'AMM et aux conclusions des rapports de validation qui ont fixé les limites des paramètres critiques.
Source Le Hir 1997: 27

TEACHING TRANSLATION WITH THE HELP OF COMPUTERS: THE ADDED VALUE OF HYPERTEXTUALITY

Marina Orsini-Jones
Coventry University

This essay will focus upon the use of technology to create an interactive pedagogic paradigm in the teaching of translation.[1] It will do so with particular reference to the teaching of translation from Italian into English. It will argue that the use of computers to teach source texts from a variety of registers enhances students' experience of such texts and makes them more aware of (a) specific features in the Italian language, (b) Italian content-related matters, especially literature and area studies, and (c) translation studies issues.

Teaching translation with the help of the computer is a rather under-represented area of studies. Even in CALL (Computer Assisted Language Learning) literature, translation assisted by the use of a computer is scarcely discussed.[2] One notable exception is, in my opinion, the best textbook about comparative Italian/English translation to date, i.e. *Translating Texts* by Margherita Ulrich. Ulrich states that it is an area enjoying tremendous success among professional translators today and that machine-aided translation (MAT) is destined to make further developments in the future. Ulrich reminds us that MAT designates translations that are generated by a human translator with the aid of a computer. Linguistic data, such as specialized terminology, bilingual dictionaries and the like, are stored in data banks and can be called up for consultation during the actual translation process at the touch of a computer key. Among the on-line computer aids which aspiring translators should become familiar with are the following:

(a) accelerated dictionary look-up (computerized dictionaries);
(b) easily activated text-related glossaries;
(c) concordance information to promote terminological consistency.[3]

The point needs emphasizing that computers cannot translate alone and that the new professional translator is one who knows how computers can help with their work:

> Whether the TT [Target Text] has been produced by a machine, a machine and a human translator, or a translator alone, it needs to fulfil the basic requirement of containing the same information content as the ST [Source Text]. The ultimate decision on its acceptability, for the time-being at least, still rests with the human translator.[4]

Although Ulrich talks only about professional translators, these days students need to acquire professional skills, and if they have to engage with translation they should do so as the professionals do. Furthermore, the Italian translation class (normally delivered to relatively small groups) provides an innovative and more democratic setting in which students can become engaged in scholarship themselves, as part of their learning experience, and can themselves create learning environments which are collaborative and 'powerful'.[5] This area is a new and exciting field in translation studies, which may counteract the pessimism expressed by Brian Farrington on the subject. Farrington pointed out that the lack of research in this area has to do with the fact that 'translation is widely discredited as a language learning activity'.[6] He ascribed this phenomenon to the negative association, wrongly made in his opinion, between the use of translation for teaching a language and the grammar/translation method, which makes the mistake of equating prose or 'unseen' translation with *learning* a foreign language. Furthermore, he argued that despite the fact that there are not many studies on translation for language learning and teaching, most HE languages departments still give this exercise a high status, and use it at the higher levels of language learning and teaching. He maintained that it should be so, as:

> If we recognize the distinction [...] between performative and cognitive knowledge of a language, or, in simpler terms, knowing the language and knowing *about* the language, we can see the learner's progression as being one in which performative knowledge is most useful in the earlier stages, cognitive knowledge only becoming important in the later. Translation is certainly, for most learners, an activity in which the cognitive dominates.[7]

Moreover, Farrington added that although we need to distinguish between translation as a way to teach language and teaching translation in itself as a distinct skill, using a computer could assist with both. In fact I maintain that using a computer to assist with teaching translation can enhance students' awareness not only about language learning, but also about translation skills and about different kinds of textualities, or, better, of hypertextualities of the text studied.

The idea of students collaborating in the creating of meaning in translation, with the help of hypertextual links on a computer is not new. Patrick Corness at Coventry University was exploring MAT as early as the mid-1980s and June and Doug Thompson at the University of Hull were developing computer-based translation materials for their students at more or less the same time.[8] With funding from the government's Training Agency, Corness received support to create courseware for commercial companies wishing to train staff in German translation: this resulted in the creation of *TIGER – Translating Industrial GERman*.[9] The first work by Corness was carried out using a word-processor but the advanced module for *TIGER* was developed in the Toolbook hypertext authoring system. With Toolbook it became possible to overcome some of the weaknesses of the word-processing package previously used and to create a robust learning environment with a windows-based screen design where the text files were stable and students could access help files at the click of a button on the screen. Italian translation-teaching at Hull was moving in a similar direction, with the development of *TransIt*.[10] The similarity of approach between *TIGER* and *TransIt* meant that a merger to take advantage of the best characteristics of both would enhance resources, and not just for the two language involved, i.e. German and Italian. Thus were created the present-day version of *TransIt* and *TransLit*, and of an Authoring Shell.[11] All three have been incorporated into the teaching, learning, and assessment of Italian-English translation at the University of Hull.[12]

The *TransIt* (technical Italian texts) and the *TransLit* (literary Italian texts) interfaces allow students to interact with a text to translate on computer and to have a variety of hypertextual help files (see Figure 1, the introductory page to *TransIt-TIGER*, and Figure 2, the alternative versions for the translation given).

On a split screen, the students engage with the text they have to translate: in the top part is the original and in the lower half the students have to type their version. While doing so they can call up a variety of help buttons: 'hints', suggestions on how to translate, little clues; 'glossary', a useful tailor-made vocabulary for each text; and 'context', extra information which helps with understanding the setting for the passage.

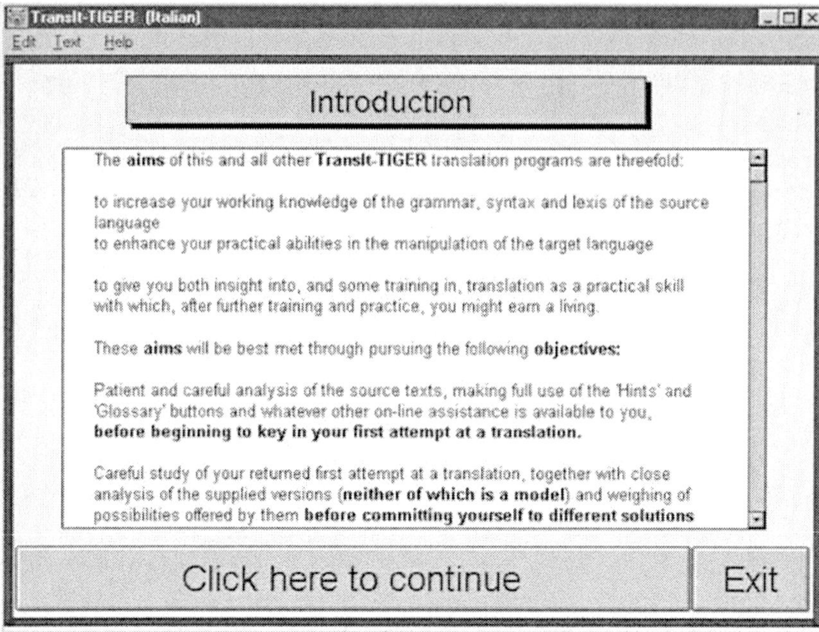

Figure 1: Introductory screen in *TransIt-TIGER*

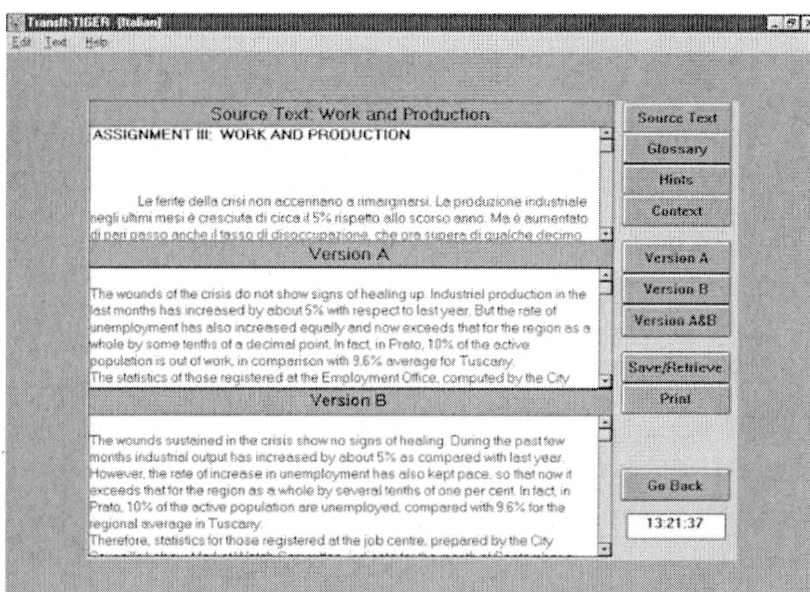

Figure 2: The split screen giving alternative versions of the translation

Obviously the context section varies considerably between *TransIt*, technical language, and *TransLit*, literary hints. After students have translated some text, they can call up the two alternative translation versions of the passage provided within the package at the touch of a button and engage in comparison/discussion of their work. In the words of June Thompson, *TransIt*:

> attempts to heighten learners' awareness of the linguistic subtleties involved in producing a good translation, and at the same time to refine their linguistic capabilities in both the source and the target languages. [...] it provides some insight into the kind of environment in which a modern professional translator operates.[13]

Having used *TransLit* with students working in pairs (each pair sharing a PC), I have observed how it triggers a healthy debate amongst them – which I incidentally force them to carry out in Italian as much as possible – about both translation alternatives, and the process of translation itself.

The *TransIt-TIGER* model was exemplary in showing how the process of translation can be enhanced by the use of a computer, and is still valid today. However, the progress made by technology in recent years requires a new approach to the teaching of MAT. The *TransIt* model was developed using the authoring software Toolbook in the years before the advent of the world wide web. The introduction into higher education of virtual learning environments (VLEs), such as WebCT and Blackboard, has added dynamism and interactivity to the way in which computers can be used for translation studies. Within VLEs, students:

(a) have additional opportunities to plan their discourse;
(b) become more reflective in their approach to language learning and linguistic production;
(c) have new opportunities of virtual communication/debate outside the allocated contact hours;
(d) have *FREE* direct access to on-line dictionaries, concordancers, glossaries, and many other www-based hypertextual tools;[14]
(e) have new opportunities to create their own hypertextual translation projects so that they themselves can provide alternative versions of a translation and discuss them on-line.

I have personally taken advantage of the new medium to make the teaching of translation more student-centred. My students can supplement their face-to-face debates in class with virtual ones on the 'discussion forum' area within the on-line learning environment we have adopted campus-wide at Coventry University, WebCT (see Figure 3, 1998–99 WebCT interface for Italian module).[15]

Furthermore, within WebCT the tutor can easily provide direct links to on-line translation tools, such as those above described by Ulrich, within the learning environment where the translation is being analysed. It is moreover relatively easy to allow students to create their own hypertextual analysis of a text to translate on-line, so that learners become entirely the 'owners' of the learning process via the creation of hypertext environments, used to teach each other translation issues. The e-discourse and the powerful on-line learning environments are, in short, radically changing the way in which we relate not only to texts, but also to the teaching of modern languages and of translation.[16]

The introduction of the 'on-line campus' at Coventry University in 1998 opened up new ways of delivering a translation course.[17] The students involved are final year undergraduates on Joint Honours BA in Modern Languages and/or European Studies programmes and Socrates students on exchange programmes. The level is advanced/higher advanced and the module bears 25% of the final year credits. The assessment for this module consists of coursework (30%), oral examination (30%), and written examination (40%). From the first academic year in which it has run (i.e. 1998–99) students have had to produce a group presentation in hypertext format about comparative English/Italian translation issues which counts for 12% of the final mark for the module.

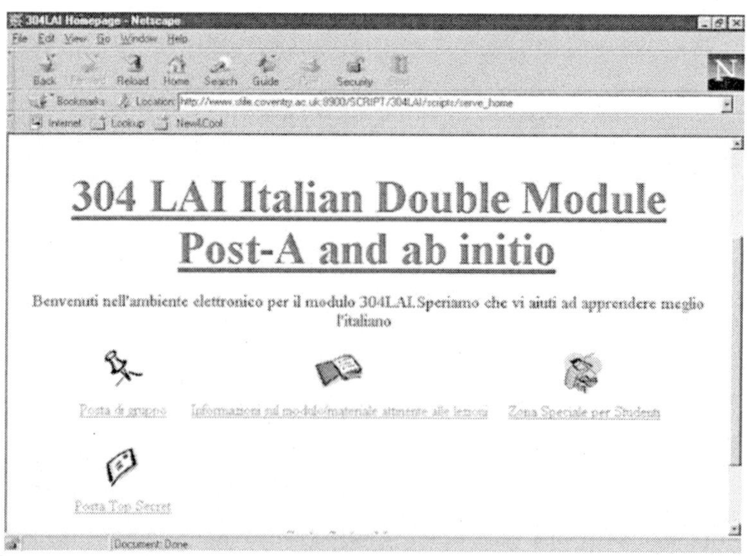

Figure 3: WebCT interface for Italian module at Coventry University

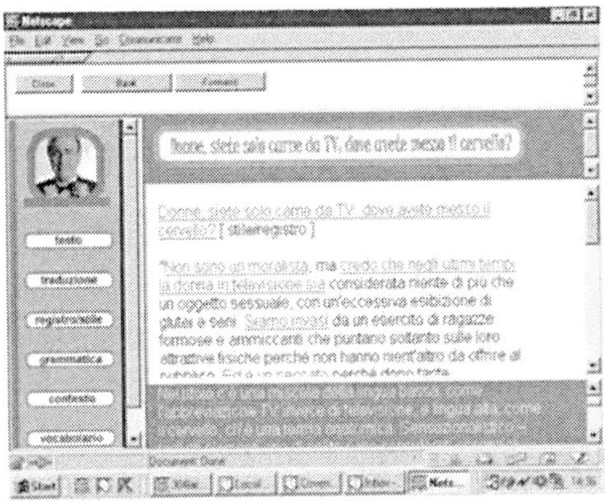

Figure 4: Student group hypertextual presentation, 1999–2000

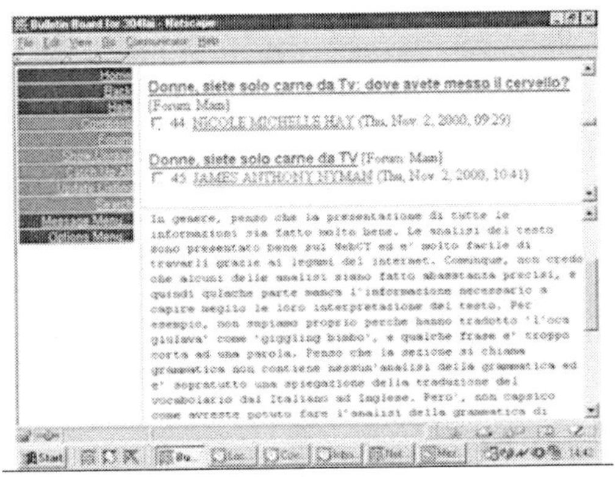

Figure 5: Students' evaluation of presentation in discussion forum, 2000-01

The contact hours are three. Two are devoted to the theory and practice of translation: staff and students start a translation in class, on paper, discussing issues relating to the translation of texts from Italian into English and vice-versa. Such discussion is underpinned by the study of some translation theory, the use of an advanced level Italian grammar book used to highlight Italian/English differences in register, style, and grammar at a high level, and translation practice/seminars. In the third hour, for the first six months, students work in the computer lab, where they share ideas about translation in discussion forum and analyse the work (the on-line presentations) done by their predecessors in previous years, evaluate it, and make suggestions on what they would have done with the same texts (see Figures 4 and 5, one of the students' presentations from academic year 1999–2000, and the students' debate about it in discussion forum, 2000–01).

In addition, students can make use of a 'resource area' with direct links to the Italian home-page, which contains information about Italian culture and society, and to the main Italian daily and weekly newspapers, and to on-line dictionaries. Homework is assigned on WebCT on a weekly basis. Students are therefore required to use WebCT regularly, not just for discussions about work done in class, but also to present their homework. Students are asked to communicate exclusively in Italian in discussion forum: they are not penalized for the mistakes they make, but their mistakes are analysed by the two tutors in charge of the module, who then choose translation texts appropriate for raising the discussion of grammar/vocabulary issues in which students have shown some weaknesses (without making it obvious to the students). Also, the two lecturers provide individual on-line feedback on grammar problems.

As for the choice of how to create categories of contrastive translation analysis to 'deconstruct' passages from Italian or English, following students' and staff's negotiation both in class and in discussion forum, texts are normally analysed for the following aspects: register, grammar/syntax, vocabulary, and context. For their assessed presentation, students, working in groups:

(a) take a brief Italian passage of their choice (normally an extract from a contemporary novel or from an article in a weekly magazine) and submit it to the lecturers for approval;
(b) once the text is approved, students translate the passage and classify the translation issues in it according to the above categories;
(c) they then create mini-descriptions in Italian of each word they want to present from the chosen passage for each category and type them in Microsoft Word;
(d) they then liaise with the technical designer to decide on the 'look' of their mini-package and to finalize the hyperlinks;
(e) once the hypertext is ready the designer liaises with the lecturers who then upload the presentation in the 'resources/contents' area of WebCT the day before the presentation is delivered;
(f) the group presentation is delivered in the computer lab, in Italian, using the package created by the students, which can be seen by everybody both on the wide-screen and on each individual PC.

In the first year of the module the initial task given to the students was to identify categories of translation issues relating to an extract from the cult novel *Jack Frusciante è uscito dal gruppo* by Enrico Brizzi, which is also available in its English translation.[19] Each group came up with their suggestions and in the end we agreed on our 'translation template' which would be used by students for their assessed presentations. In the following years, instead of negotiating a new format, we evaluated what students from previous years had done so that, effectively, students were learning mainly from their peers.

In the second year, 1999–2000, most students produced work which was varied and very creative, and the bank of 'translation studies' created by the students is growing bigger, as different cohorts of students contribute to its on-going development.[20] All students seem to have developed further their analytical skills and the positive feedback at the end of the module indicates that most are also happy with the acquisition of intertextual skills, together with ICT skills. The module is therefore becoming truly interactive: the negotiation of textual meaning is carried out almost exclusively by students for other students and 'kept for posterity' within WebCT. The original texts are re-visited by students and transformed into hypertexts. Students, in so doing, 'appropriate' the text.

George Landow points out that although the electronic linking disperses text into other texts, the process does not weaken and/or destroy its *hypertextual* uniqueness.[21] On the contrary, careful structuring of the navigation within a hypertext enhances the students' perception of the 'main' text as the focal point of their analysis. At the same time students will feel free to deconstruct, break, scatter, and re-construct context according to their needs. Hypertext is inherently flexible and has the property of metamorphosing into what the learner/reader and/or lecturer want out of it. Landow notes that hypertext takes power away from the lecturer and re-directs it to the student (from the methodological point of view) and from the author to the reader (from the philosophical point of view) and his point is undeniable.

I maintain that the use of hypertextuality within a context of negotiated learning carried out both face-to-face and on-line enhances students' analytical skills and enables the lecturer(s) to teach at the same time the language, translation theory, and related content (whether literary or not) in a modern foreign language. In order to do so, however, the relationships between lecturers, students, and computers must become more fluid. For effective learning to take place a democratization of roles must take place too. I have already illustrated how this can be done when describing the way I had integrated a CD-ROM into the teaching of Italian language and society in a second year module.[22] To summarize briefly, the model which grew out of the integration of the CD-ROM into my teaching is the following: the Fluid Role Exchange Environment (*FREE*), represents a flexible and interactive 'pool' where the three main actors, i.e. the learner, the lecturer, and the computer, exchange roles. The paradigm described in the *FREE* is meant to be constructivist with reference to the permanent contribution to both the design and learning process which students' feedback brings in.[23]

The use of WebCT added an extra dimension to the *FREE* model since the student-designed learning environments are kept for future cohorts of students on the same module. This creates 'ripples' of student-centred on-line learning and on-line debate about translation studies from one year to the other. The computer is not a mere 'tool' any longer, as it enables human-to-human communication and interaction, something the microcomputers of the 1980s or the PCs of the late 1980s and early 1990s could not do. The machine therefore becomes a 'hypertool' and enhances the learning environment by adding to it the dynamism of interactive hypertextuality, of ongoing peer-review and of students' own reflections made visible in written form in discussion forum. Furthermore, my experience over the last three academic years shows that the hypertextual group projects in Italian have also enhanced students' motivation and commitment. The experience of integrating a VLE into my translation course has resulted in an updated version of the *FREE* (Fluid Role Evolving Environment) model, a more dynamic one, developed in collaboration with Anne Davidson, a colleague from Health and Social Sciences. The *FREE* through WebCT (Figure 6) better reflects the way in which the 'hypertool' has enhanced the learning environment by magnifying its hypertextual resonance year after year.

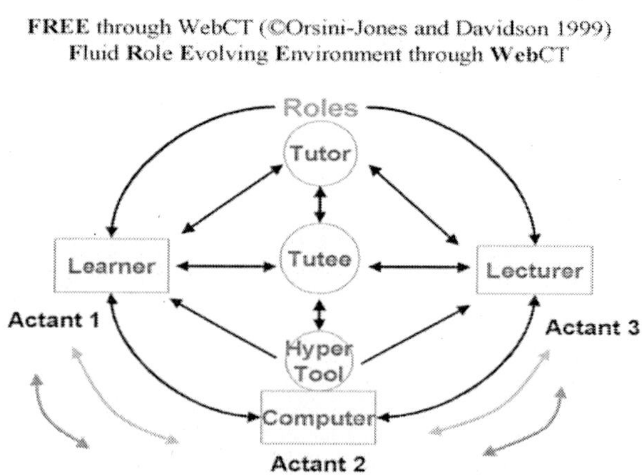

Figure 6: FREE through WebCT

NOTES

1 It must be pointed out that this essay will not deal with the topic of machine translation using artificial intelligence systems, as, for example, in *Computers in Translation*, ed. J. Newton (London: Routledge, 1992).
2 There is no mention of it in Michael Levy's highly-regarded *Computer Assisted Language Learning* (Oxford: Clarendon Press, 1997).
3 M. Ulrich, *Translating Texts* (Rapallo: Cideb, 1992), p. 24.
4 Ulrich, *Translating Texts*, p. 25.
5 See E. De Corte, 'Fostering Cognitive Growth: A Perspective from Research on Mathematics', *Educational Psychologist*, 30 (1995), 37–46. See also M. Orsini-Jones and G. Cousin, 'Focus Research in Modern Languages: Creating a "Powerful Learning Environment" for Students with Students', in *Language-Learning Futures: Issues and Strategies for Modern Languages Provision in Higher Education*, ed. J. A. Coleman *et al.* (London: CILT/SCHML 2001, pp. 71–82).
6 B. Farrington, 'Translation and the Microcomputer', in *Computers in Applied Linguistics and Language Teaching*, ed. U. O. H. Jung, (Frankfurt am Main: P. Lang, 1991), p. 119.
7 Farrington, 'Translating and the Microcomputer', p. 120.
8 Patrick Corness described how he approached CAT (Computer Assisted Translation, an alternative to MAT) in the paper 'Three Aspects of Information Technology Applications to Language Learning: Translation, Grammar and Dialogues' given in Beijing at the 1997 Sino-British Conference on Multimedia Applications in English Language Teaching.
9 P. J. Corness, F. H. Deepwell, and C. R. Daniels, *TIGER: Advanced Module* (Coventry: Coventry University, 1992).
10 D. Thompson and J. Thompson, 'Advanced (Technical) Translation (Italian/English): a Pilot Project', *Language Learning with Computers*, eds. P. Baumgartner and A. Hall (Klagenfurt: WISL, 1991).
11 D. Thompson, J. Thompson, P. J. Corness, and F. H. Deepwell, *TransIt-TIGER and TransLit-TIGER* (Hull: TELL/Hodder and Stoughton/The University of Hull, 1997).
12 See J. Thompson, 'Embedding Technology into Language Examinations: A Case Study', *Active Learning*, 4 (1996), 24–29.
13 J. Thompson, 'Embedding Technology into Language Examinations', p. 24.
14 For the concept of *FREE*, see below, note 22.
15 See the site of the Coventry University Centre for Higher Education Development at http://193.61.107.61/ched.
16 See also T. Connell, 'Web Support for Distance Learning in the Field of Translation', *ReCALL*, 11, no. 2 (1999), 31–37. The process of change in the teaching of the humanities caused by the advent of sophisticated technological tools has been thoroughly analysed by M. Rifaterre in his 'Intertextuality vs Hypertextuality', *New Literary History*, 25 (1995), 779–88.
17 See M. Orsini-Jones and A. Davidson, 'From Reflective Learners to Reflective Lecturers via WebCT', *Active Learning*, 10 (1999), 33–38, and M. Orsini-Jones, 'Implementing Institutional Change for Languages: On-line Collaborative Learning Environments at Coventry University', *ReCALL*, 11, no. 2 (1999), 67–84.
18 The book we use is M. Dalla Casa, *Costruire la lingua* (Brescia: La Scuola, 1993).
19 E. Brizzi, *Jack Frusciante è uscito dal gruppo* (Milan: Mondadori, 1994) and E. Brizzi, *Jack Frusciante Has Left the Band* (London: HarperCollins-Flamingo, 1998).
20 Orsini-Jones, 'Implementing Institutional Change for Languages'.
21 N.B., not *textual*, as in Landow. See G. P. Landow, *Hypertext: the Convergence of Contemporary Critical Theory and Technology* (Baltimore: Johns Hopkins University Press, 1992).
22 For further details on the model and the CD-ROM, see M. Orsini-Jones and D. Jones, 'Hypermedia for Language Learning: The *FREE* Model at Coventry University', *Association for Learning Technology Journal*, 4, no. 2 (1996), 28–39 and M. Orsini-Jones and V. Tandy, *La neve nel bicchiere: A Multimedia CD-Rom for Students of Italian* (Coventry: Coventry University/Camsoft, 1998).

COMPUTERIZED SUBTITLING: A MULTIMODAL APPROACH TO THE LEARNING OF MINORITY LANGUAGES

Anthony Baldry
University of Pavia

There is a growing awareness that if European society is to function successfully, multilingual skills involving at least a receptive knowledge of Europe's lesser-studied languages will be necessary. The *New Information Technologies* project of the Council for Cultural Co-operation, launched in 1999 in response to the mandate of the second Summit of Heads of State and Government, established the likelihood that these skills will be acquired in relation to emerging technologies, in particular, digital television:

> The number of commonly available television channels has increased from a few to dozens in the space of a decade. In the next few years, digital broadcasting will increase that number to hundreds. [...] European cultural industries and artists have, however, been slow to respond to the challenge. [...] The work undertaken by the Council of Europe should identify means to promote creative expression for all groups, *including minority groups, communication in lesser-used languages*, and activities developing the cultural visibility of smaller European countries, particularly in Central and Eastern Europe.
> (http://culture.coe.fr/postsummit/nti/en/eproject.htm, my italics)

Perhaps less widely known, or indeed developed, is the use of subtitling in relation to language learning, which has been explicitly mentioned by the Council of Europe on a number of occasions in the context of minority languages.[1] Under the 1992 European Charter for Regional or Minority Languages (Straßburg/Strasbourg, 5.XI.1992), the signatory parties:

> Realising that the protection and promotion of regional or minority languages in the different countries and regions of Europe represent an important contribution to the building of a Europe based on the principles of democracy and cultural diversity [undertook] to foster the different means of access in other languages to works *produced in regional or minority languages* by aiding and developing translation, dubbing, post-synchronisation *and subtitling activities.* (http://book.coe.fr/conv/en/ets/148-en.htm, my italics)

Little as yet seems to have been done to link up subtitled film media and emerging technologies in such a way as to implement self-access language-learning courses. In particular, no computer-based on-line course using simultaneous subtitling in both English and a minority language appears to have been developed for the acquisition of receptive skills in any of the European Union's minority languages, even though computer-based subtitling is potentially an effective way of overcoming the first 'make-it-or-break-it' stages of listening and reading comprehension, in which it is still hard to recognize the individual words in an interactional encounter. Clearly, a case can be made for European ODL, CALL, and Language Learning Centres to come together to set up an on-line Internet service under which self-access users, many of them home-based, will be able to find motivating subtitled materials relating to the learning of minority languages.

In this context, subtitling may be viewed as a highly specialized co-contextualizing force facilitating the self-access acquisition of receptive skills in minority languages. A subtitle exists, of course, to assist interpretation of another text, but the requirement, proposed here, of simultaneous reading of texts in L1 and L2, as well as listening to texts in L2, brings into play textual processes that are rather more complex than is the case even with the majority of L1/L2 and script/dialogue combinations for language-learning purposes found in intralingual subtitling, interlingual subtitling, and reversed subtitling.[2] With due experimentation, this use of subtitling may prove to be an important source of motivation when attempting to access other minority language text types which, according to the social circumstances, presuppose a different 'mix' of receptive skills such as listening to a car radio, reading a newspaper, or combinations of reading and listening skills found in lectures or business briefings.

Experimentation to test the validity of this model goes, however, beyond the purposes of the present paper. Here the focus is instead on the tools, conceptual and technological, that support the research and development underlying the possible implementation of the very first stages in the production of an on-line Internet service of the type mentioned above. In particular, the paper seeks to provide a working hypothesis answering a basic question, namely: in what way does computerized subtitling require our current assumptions about subtitling to be redefined? The main focus in this paper is thus on providing a preliminary sketch of the differences between computerized subtitling for language-learning purposes and subtitling for entertainment purposes. This involves a series of textual comparisons and analyses best illustrated in relation to a familiar media text, namely Roberto Benigni's film *La vita è bella* (*Life is beautiful*).[3]

Christopher Taylor writes that 'subtitles must [...] attempt to bring the language plane and the non-linguistic plane together where necessary to relay meaning'.[4] But unlike subtitling for entertainment purposes, rather than a single continuous showing of the film, subtitling for language learning presupposes a staged, cyclic access with the *same* sequence being viewed on each occasion with *different* overlays. This creates a more complex relationship between subtitle and film text and hence a greater need to understand how the source text works than we might otherwise expect when subtitling a film.[5] Figure 1 is a specialized form of multimodal transcription containing a series of frames that reconstruct a scene in the opening sequence of Benigni's film where the hero, a waiter named Guido Orefice, pretends to be a prince.[6] The transcription helps interpret the way resources build up the micro and macro features of a text. Thus, apart from a visual frame, the transcription records what was actually heard (L: = language, M: = music, S: = sound), seen (VF: = visual focus, gaze), and done (G: = gesture, Movt: = movement, body posture), suggesting that the integration of these resources is an important source of meaning (Column 3). The transcription also reconstructs the subtitling used in a commercially-available subtitled version of the film (Column 2, top of each row) comparing it with an alternative set of (italicized) L2 subtitles (Column 2, bottom of each row) proposed for language-learning purposes which, as exemplified in Figure 2, are coupled in the resubtitled film with the (italicized) L1 subtitles in Column 3. As well as including visual frames, the first column subdivides the text into blocks of 1, 2, or 3 seconds (instantiated as rows in a table), each corresponding to a shot (defined as 'a filmed visual sequence in which there is no spatial displacement of the camera').[7] The notation L(1) and L(2) in Columns 2 and 3, indicates cases where two sets of subtitles are shown within the same time frame. Before we look into the differences between the two sets of subtitles it is helpful to define the scene's role in the structure of the film.

The scene is, in fact, the third and final part of the film's 'prologue'

T	Subtitled frames	Subtitles used & proposed	Soundtrack	Visual resources
1 - 2		I'm washing my hands. (1) *–I'm going to wash my hands* (2) *– Bravo*	L (1): - *Mi vado a lavare le mani* L (2) (amico): - *Bravo* M: changes from clarinet to trombone	Transition to new phase starts G: Material action: (arm hand pointing to where he intends to wash his hands)
3 - 4		Untitled *[(2) – Bravo]*	 M: trombone	VF: on walking G: Material action: hangs up coat near pump
5		Untitled *Noise of the pump*	S: *Rumore della pompa* (sound of the pump) M: ceases	Transition complete G: Material action: (pumping)
6 - 7		Untitled *Sound of water*	*Rumore di acqua* S: Sound of water	New phase G: Material action: (hand washing)
8		Untitled *Sound of water*	S: *Rumore di acqua* (sound of water)	VF: Girl milking cow; [Textual Metafunction: Given information in the soundtrack; New in the visual]
9 - 12		Pretty girl! How's it going *Hey there young lady!* *How are things? Ehm?*	L: *Oilà bella bambina!* *Come va? Eh?*	G: Material action: (hand washing) Gaze: looks at girl
13		What are you doing? *What are you doing?*	L: *Che stai facendo?*	VF: Material action: (right to centre walk: oblique angle)
14 - 16		Did your mom put this stuff here? (1) *Just look at all these lovely things!* (2) *Who put them there, your mummy?*	L (1): *Ma guarda quanta bella roba* L (2): *Chi ce l'ha messo, la mamma?*	VF: on the cart Movt: walks towards the cart
17 - 18		No, the landlady, did. *-No the lady I do jobs for did* *-The lady you do jobs for?*	L (1) (Eleonora): *No la padroncina!* L (2): *La padroncina?*	VF: as before
19 - 20		Is it a market? It's beautiful. (1) *Just look at this! Now is it a market?!* (2) *How beautiful it is!*	L(1): *Ma guarda! Ma che è un mercato?!* L(2): *Ma è una cosa bellissima!*	VF: as before
21 - 23		How much is it? How old are you? (1) *Can you buy? How much is it?* (2) *And how old are you? Where's your mummy?*	L(1): *Si può comprare? Quanto costa?* L(2): *E quanti anni hai? Dov'è la mamma?*	VF: frames the two participants as discourse partners
24 - 25		Untitled *I've asked you too many questions.* *- What's your name*	L(1) (off screen voice): *T'ho fatto troppe domande!* L (2) (off screen voice): *Come ti chiami?*	VF: first cut to girl's face Gaze: girl's intense scrutiny of the newcomer

T	Subtitled frames	Subtitles used & proposed	Soundtrack	Visual resources
26		-What's your name? -Eleanora *Eleanora*	L: (Eleonora): *Eleonora*	VF: frames the two participants as discourse partners
27 - 28		Nice to meet you I'm prince Guido. (1) *Pleased to meet you* (2) *Prince Guido*	L (1): *Molto piacere.* L(2): *Principe Guido*	VF: on one participant G: material process: hand-arm movement to remove hat
29 - 31		-Prince? -I'm a prince, I am prince?? - *Prince?* - *(Of course) I'm a prince*	L: (Eleonora) *Principe?* *Sono un principe* (off screen)	VF: focus on the girl's response Gaze: girl's facial expression casts doubt on the claim to be a prince
32		-Prince? -I'm a prince?, I am *Didn't you know?*	L: *Non lo saperi?*	VF: frames the two participants as discourse partners. G: material process: hand-arm movement to replace hat
33 - 34		All this is mine 1) *Here everything's mine, you know. Oh!* 2) *Here everything's mine*	L(1): *Qui è tutto mio. Sai. Oh!* L(2): *Qui è tutto mio*	VF: as before G: right hand-arm stretched out to create a distance-reducing link between the participants
35 - 38		Here starts the prince's principate *From here proceeds the principality of the prince. Uh.*	L: *Qui é il principio del principato del principe. Eh..*	VF: as before G: as before
39 - 40		I'll call this place Addis Ababa *This place.. I'll call it …* *Mmm….Addis Ababa*	L: *Questo posto lo chiamerò... Addis Abeba*	G: Finger on lips [i.e. a mental process precedes a verbal process]
41 - 42		I'll change it all. Out go the cows. In come the camels. *I'll change everything here, I will.*	L: (said as an off screen voice) *Cambio tutto qua, io.*	VF: Cut to young girl Gaze: Given information (face as before, whereas the New is in the off-screen linguistic info.)
43 - 44		I'll change it all. Out go the cows. In come the camels. (1) *Out with the cows, in with the camels* (2) *Out with the hens, in with the ostriches*	L(1): *Via le mucche e tutti i cammelli.* L(2) *Via le galline e tutti gli struzzi* S: clucking sound of hens	VF: frames the two participants as discourse partners G: Sweep of hand instantiates the complete material process of removal of animals
45 - 46		Camels? *Ostriches and camels?*	L (E): *Struzzi e cammelli?*	VF: cut to young girl Gaze: as before: no smile and rather quizzical
47 - 48		Even a few hippopotamus. *And a few hippos too* *(nervous laughter)*	L: *E anche qualche ippopotamo…(risatina)*	VF: frames participants as discourse partners

T	Subtitled frames	Subtitles used & proposed	Soundtrack	Visual resources
49 - 50		I must go I'm meeting with the princess (1) *Bye I'm off…* (2) *…'cause I'm meeting the princess*	L (1): *Ciao. Vado via …* L (2): *…perché ho l'appuntamento con la principessa*	VF: as before G : left-hand-arm is retracted signalling intent to leave
51 - 52		- When - Now - *When?* - *Now!*	L (Eleonora): - *Quando?* - *Ora!*	VF: cut to young girl Gaze: as before: no smile and rather quizzical
53 - 54		Untitled *Ouch! Oooooouch!*	L/S: (female voice): *Ay!* *….Ay! Ay! Ay!:* M: starts up softly	Transition: Gaze: E. looks up anticipating new camera angle and a new viewer/viewed relationship
55 - 56		Untitled -*Aah!* -*Hey!*	L/S: (female voice): *Oooh* *Hey* M:	Transition to new phase continues Movt: Pigeons fly out
57 - 58		Untitled *Gasp of surprise*	L/S: *fa un sospiro pieno di sorpresa* M: cymbals clash	New phase: Body posture: The 'vertical' position of the previous phase becomes 'horizontal'
59 - 60		Good morning. Princess! *Good morning. Princess!*	L: *Buon giorno principessa* M: a romantic melody strikes up	VF: frames participants as discourse partners Body posture: the two bodies begin to separate

Figure 1: A multimodal transcription contextualizing L1 and L2 subtitling

and as such heralds the attempt, which will be made in the film, to preserve the innocence and beauty of childhood, despite the forces of death and Fascism. The scene, shot on a bright sunny day, has a fairy-tale quality that contrasts with what precedes and follows, namely: (a) a Bergmanesque opening scene portraying a shadowy figure in an impenetrable, foggy background in which an off-screen speaker establishes that this will be a tale of sorrow but also a fable containing moments of happiness and joy; and (b) a scene in which the sinister, uncaring world of politics is portrayed in a night-time shot of political posters featuring Mussolini fleetingly glimpsed in car headlights.

The advantage of a multimodal transcription is that it reconstructs the film director's storyboard revealing how sounds and gestures that are easily overlooked are, in fact, essential to the construction of the story. In the opening scenes, they often have a cataphoric function pointing to and anticipating what will happen in the rest of the film. Benigni's character Guido spins the yarn that he is off to meet the princess and lo and behold the Princess falls from the sky, thus maintaining the film's basic textual characteristic of a fairy tale in which what is promised *will* be fulfilled. Indeed, in the film's climax, the promise contained in the life-preserving version of the game of hide-and-seek that Guido plays with his son, in which the first to score a 1000 points will win a tank, comes to be fulfilled precisely by the arrival of an American tank. The game, and its eventual outcome, has, of course, one meaning for the innocent son and another for the audience.

These dual meanings, a constant feature of the film, are established multimodally through the combined use of gesture, the human body, and the word. Thus, in the second scene of the film, which immediately precedes this one, Guido's car careers down the road, its brakes having failed, and risks mowing down the crowd waiting for the king to arrive. He waves desperately and shouts 'via' to clear the road, an action which is taken by the crowd as a Fascist salute, thus superimposing two meanings, one for the crowd, which responds with cries of 'viva', and another for today's cinema audience who sees the irony in the 'via'/'viva' contrast and in the hand-arm salute with its various levels of significance. The arm salute combines a salute (deference) to the king with a warning to avoid the runaway car, plus, of course, the Fascist salute, and is ambiguously and multiply contextualized across these three domains. These domains are, of course, contradictory in the larger context of the film: a celebration of the joy of life (which is also mindful of the people who could be run over by the car) is contrasted with royal power and complicity with life-denying Fascism. The salute in the runaway-car scene heralds the fact that the film as well as a fable is also a political allegory, a matter further developed in the current scene through the reference to Addis Ababa which, as well as fantasy and exotica, also connotes colonial power. The scene cements the relationship between fable and political allegory, the world of play and fantasy and the grimmer realities, which will be thematized at many points in the film. The Fascist castles in the air invoking colonial fantasies and ambitions are indeed a reference point for the pretend prince's own fantasies. At the same time, the scene also relates to the interpersonal negotiation between Guido and the girl. It involves an encounter between two disparate perspectives which have to be negotiated against the backcloth of the other aspects of the film which multimodally contextualize these two standpoints and the relations between them. The scene thus establishes links between individuals and society that are crucial to the build-up of the film's thematics.

Even a partial and incomplete multimodal analysis such as the one given here shows how many of the meanings in this scene, like the majority in this film, are intensely interpersonal in nature and hence why subtitling for language-learning purposes needs to reflect this. The subtitles on the left-hand side of Column 2 (Figure 1) designed for purely entertainment purposes fail to draw attention to a number of crucial resources used to build up aspects of interpersonal engagement and negotiation. These include: (a) minor clauses, such as 'ma guarda' and 'via'; (b) voice prosodics, ranging from the shouted 'oilà' to the slightly hushed and confidential 'non lo sapevi'; (c) gesture, ranging from violent hand-and-arm waving to more introspective touching of the lips; (d) the background sounds, ranging from soothing music and water splashing to alarmed hen clucking and cries of pain.

A comparison of the two sets of subtitles helps clarify that they foreground very different meanings. Quite apart from its other functions, the scene has the primary goal of describing two very different first encounters between individuals: the first relates to a fanciful storyteller meeting a captive audience (the young lady), the second to Prince Guido's first encounter with his princess. As such, the predominant focus might be expected, even in cinema subtitling, to be on interpersonal meaning. But subtitles such as 'Here starts the prince's principate', typical of expository rather than conversational style, fail to convey the wordplay present in the original 'Qui è il principio del principato del principe', designed to impress a suitably gawping audience. It is at least partly captured by 'From here proceeds the principality of the prince'. This example highlights just how far cinema subtitling is concerned with *what* is said rather than the *way* it is said, a reflection of a well-established procedure whereby the professional subtitler strips out as much of the interpersonal and the textual as possible and leaves only the ideational.[9] But, as Figure 2 suggests, this is inappropriate in the first stages of language learning where there is a need to create associations between L1 and L2 words and expressions. Interpersonal elements have been given prominence in the language-

Figure 2: Captioning and subtitling for language-learning purposes

learning version of the subtitles: the cheerfully phatic 'oilà', previously omitted, has been introduced and identified with 'Hey there', an

9-13: (1) *Oilà*: phatic: minor clause: interpersonal bid to establish contact across physical and interpersonal distance by hailing the girl; *bella bambina*: originally translated as 'pretty girl' despite the fact that the focal point is not the physical appearance of the girl but the desire to establish interpersonal contact with her. The meaning has more to do with *simpatia* hence the subtitle 'young lady'. (2) *Eh?*: interpersonal vocalization with rising intonation seeking/soliciting contact or response from the girl (originally omitted, now restored).

14-16: (1) *Ma guarda*: exclamative clause of positive affect, childlike delight in the things he sees, seeking contact with the young girl through indication of his delight, enthusiasm ('Just look at all these lovely things!'). 'Stuff' in the commercial version does not seem appropriate here; (2) *Chi ce l'ha messo, la mamma?*: 'Yes/no' interrogative in the commercial subtitle ('Did your mom put this stuff here?') when the Italian is a *wh*-interrogative in which *la mamma* is *new* information whereas the commercial subtitle turns 'your mom' into *given* information, failing to capture the interplay between the diverse worlds of the interactants which derives from very different knowledge and assumptions about interpersonal relations and how the world works. The new subtitle ('Who put them there, your mummy?') restores the Italian structure.

17-18: *No, la padrocina*: negates through polarity and lexis the assumptions made by Prince Guido. The contrast between the intimate tenor implied by *la mamma* and the formal tenor of *la padrocina* indexes the different social provenance of the two interlocutors. Also, the girl's use of the diminutive morpheme suffix '*ina*' indexes her social-interpersonal proximity to the world to which the *padrocina* class belongs. In the context of the 'market', the reference to work ('The lady I do jobs for') seems more appropriate to one of ownership ('The landlady').

19-24: *Ma guarda! Ma che è un mercato! Ma è una cosa bellissima! Si può comprare? Quanto costa? E quanti anni hai? Dov'è la mamma? T'ho fatto troppe domande!*: A concentrated series of exclamations and interrogatives all signalling Prince Guido's affect and appreciation in a childlike way; in 23 the focus shifts from the things he sees to the girl (*quanti anni hai?*) and in 24 this frenetic high-paced series of clauses, establishing contact directly by indicating appreciation, is ironically undercut by the awareness that he has asked too many questions, some of which require personal responses not perhaps justified by the limited nature of the interpersonal contact between them. The *entire* series is re-established in the new subtitling.

25-31: Guido asks the girl her name after a long series of 'inappropriate' questions. In 28 this concession to the *real* interpersonal status yields to his fantastic hyperbolic self-presentation as Prince Guido. The girl's disbelief is indicated in the interpersonally weighted voice/visual prosodics of her response in 29: '*Prince?*' + frown: effectively means 'How can that be?'

32: *non lo sapevi?*: introduced when the girl does not accept he is a prince, this interrogative semantically contains an implicit assumption which he invites the girl to accept, i.e., that he most certainly *is* a prince. Omitted in the original subtitling, despite the force of the negative polarity, which carries the assumptive meaning, i.e., 'of course you know I'm a prince'. The girl's options at this point are to go along with this or to explicitly challenge the assumption.

33-34: redundancy deriving from his fancy footwork such that he has to think double quick after nearly stumbling (linguistically) because the game races ahead of the language.

39-40: 'This place, I'll call it': Notice the hesitation in the verbal as gesture (fingers on lips) mentally preformulates the verbal showing the cross-modal link between the two modalities.

41-48: again the game races ahead and Prince Guido can not keep it up. His discourse breaks down into a series of nervous little laughs. Human sounds (including laughter and pain) and natural sounds (water and machines) usually omitted in subtitles for entertainment are typically included in multimodal language-learning subtitles given their interpersonal significance.

Figure 3: Grammatical structures that build up interpersonal meaning

English equivalent encouraging learners to identify with both the wording and the spirit of the film.

Figure 3 summarizes the way basic grammatical structures are used in this scene to build up interpersonal relationships. In so doing, it provides a critical exposition of how the original subtitling fails to recognize the way interpersonal meaning is built up. It clarifies how the scene makes constant use of questions whose grammatical form might lead us to assume they are of the information-seeking type but which in fact, with a few exceptions, are essentially phatic. That is to say, they are designed to establish contact with the child by provocatively denying her any (initial) chance of response: 'Ma guarda! Ma che è un mercato?! Ma è una cosa bellissima! Si può comprare? Quanto costa? E quanti anni hai? Dov'è la mamma? T'ho fatto troppe domande!'

In this respect, the learning procedure in a computer-based course of subtitled language materials might be as follows: a first pass through the scene with subtitles in English, a second viewing with parallel-text subtitles followed by a third viewing in which captioning of the type suggested in Figure 2 is used, a fourth viewing including intertitles which point the learner to the structures that need to be learnt. The term 'subtitles' is thus taken in this paper to include captioning and intertitling. Their function, as well as giving information about the text and stimulating memorization, is to encourage reflection on the minority language through multiple viewings.[10]

How can we encourage the use of subtitles to carry out the all-important 'reflection on language' function in other ways? One answer lies in linking them to the prefabricated multimodal blocks found in any film text. In this respect, John Sinclair has pointed out that the language we produce contains many prefabricated items such as set phrases, collocations, certain ways of expressing facts and ideas.[11] This principle is clearly extendable beyond language to actions and events in a film which contain common elements and patterns.[12] Typically in films, a textual mechanism comes into play in which multimodal meaning-making blocks get built up, partly by repetition and partly by integration with other blocks, so as to make them *salient.* It is this mechanism that typically allows films to go beyond what is possible in daily life. It is particularly prominent in *La vita è bella* where there is a gradual build-up in which a rather ordinary daily event turns into one with special, often symbolic, meanings. It is essential to the construction of the hybrid genre, part fable and part political allegory, which the film instantiates. This is the case, for example, with the act of doffing and donning hats, normal enough in the scene we have analysed (row 32, Figure 1), but part of a chain which acquires increasingly unexpected meanings. It reaches a climax in the makeshift headscarf (and skirt) that Guido dons in the final scenes, transforming himself into a woman, in an attempt to break down the barriers in the concentration camp that prevent men and women from mixing. Much the same is true regarding the interplay between apparently simple actions such as bowing, cycling, holding out one's arms, hiding and talking, all of which come to be interrelated in complex and striking cross-modal ways. As the film progresses, for example, the background theme music becomes foregrounded, to the point where it becomes part of the thematic development. It becomes a bridge overcoming the separations imposed by Fascism that climaxes in the concentration camp scene where Guido plays this music through the camp tannoy system, thereby making the impossible (sending a message of love to his wife), possible. But the music is itself tightly integrated with other semiotic modalities, in particular the act of gazing at the princess, sometimes close up, more often than not from afar.

Precisely because of the significance that the continued recycling and reworking of multimodal units may have in the textual organization of films, we need to incorporate them into the language-learning process. In recent years, the process of consolidating structures, a long-established feature of language-learning courses, has taken on a new significance with the advent of electronic corpora and electronic concordancing techniques. In principle at least, these allow learners to decide for themselves whether a particular language instance should be related, by a search in a corpus, to other instances and to general patterns. This suggests the need, in the computer-based language-learning course proposed, for tools that identify the multimodal blocks that we have described above. Such tools will allow the language learner, who has come to grips with a particular scene (such as the one transcribed in Figure 1), to focus on understanding the ways in which the specific actions, and, of course, the language used in a particular sequence, come to be re-used throughout the text.

The *MCA* (*Multimodal Corpora Authoring*) system developed in Pavia as part of the *Linguatel* project is an on-line system that allows researchers and language learners alike to establish and explore such patterns along multimodal lines. In the case indicated in Figure 4, a search has been made for the word 'principessa' and two sequences have been returned (others are off screen) in which the search word is characterized in terms of a (rather elementary) multimodal unit involving three semiotic modalities: language, subtitle, and gesture.

By clicking on the play buttons on the left of the screen the learner is able to view and hear the precise sequence in which the word appears.[14] For example, in the case of the second sequence, the learner will see the scene in the theatre in which Prince Guido uses finger movements coupled with the whispered words 'Dai guardami principessa' to enchant his princess and (successfully) cause her to look in his direction.

An analysis of all the sequences returned as a result of this search (including the ones not contained in Figure 4) will show how the term 'principessa' is used in conjunction with specialized gestures (catching the princess as she falls, using fingers to entrance her, taking his hat off to her, etc.). This helps, as we would expect in any self-respecting fairy tale, to build up the principle that the remote, the improbable, and the downright impossible *will* become the order of the day. In actual practice, more complex searches than the one shown in Figure 4, which include voice quality, visual prosodics, music, body movements, and body position, help us to understand the way in which blocks of meaning are built up into chains that trigger the perception of events as predestined by some superior force: magical powers in a make-believe world of princes and princesses that the participants only partially control. Particularly memorable in this respect is the scene in which Prince Guido, incapable of controlling his bicycle and despite his shouts of 'via' and arm-waving (cf. the runaway-car scene), ends up flattening his princess and greeting her, as in his first encounter and in many other sequences in the film, with a glowing 'Buon giorno, principessa'.

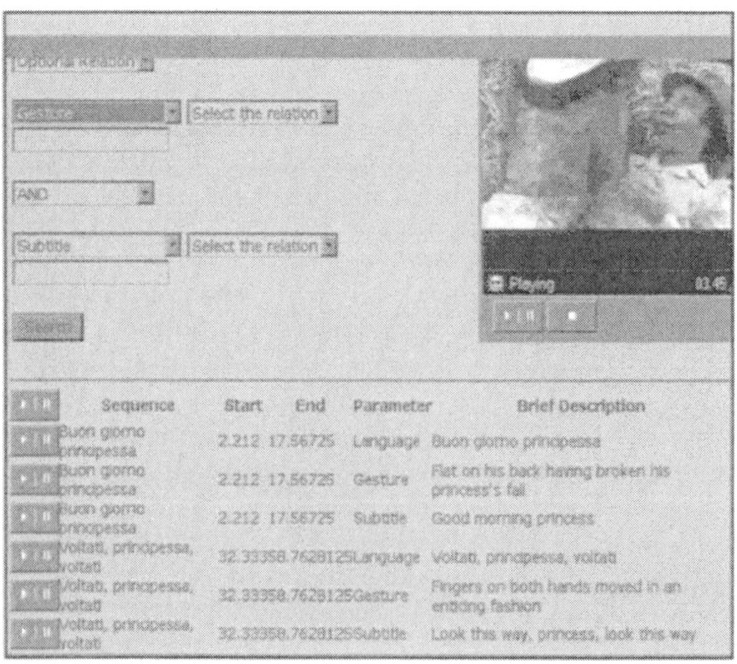

Figure 4: A multimodal concordance for *principessa* in relation to gesture

In describing research into on-line multimodal corpus (i.e. a system which allows a film to be split up virtually into sequences, tagged, and accessed as if it were a corpus), we should notice that some of our assumptions about subtitles have changed. Specifically (a), as Figure 4 shows, subtitles have been accessed paradigmatically as well as sequentially; (b) rather than as an overlay, they have been displayed as a juxtaposition to the text they describe; (c) their essentially multimodal and co-contextualizing nature is foregrounded and given a 'new spin' in relation to the macrotext: that is, we no longer assume subtitles to be isolated pieces of microtext, but view them instead in terms of sets that relate to each other in multiple ways. This is entirely in keeping with the goals and methods of language learning. Thanks to a relational database organized along multimodal principles, a search for frequent processes and events such as staring, crawling under tables, dancing on them, and (at least in this film!) riding bareback on green horses, all of which are *per se* essentially non-linguistic, can become a means to accessing and linking up linguistic data, L1 and L2 subtitles included. Thus we need no longer search *directly* for linguistic expressions of, for example, hiding as we would with traditional concordancing, but instead *indirectly* through the visual, the gestural, and so on, thereby obtaining a much wider set of linguistic expressions for this act than might otherwise be the case. We should also notice that we have taken a few steps on the road that leads from *static* forms of multimodal transcription (Figure 2) to ones which are *dynamic* (Figure 4).[15] This, in its turn, is a very small step on the road to the integration of courseware and corpusware approaches to language learning. Such integration, though providing a better balance between micro- and macro-level learning strategies, still remains a dream that is a long way from being fulfilled.[16] Whatever the timetable for these developments may prove to be, a new conception of subtitling, no longer seen as a fixed, direct, one-to-one relationship between an L2 written microtext and an L1 spoken microtext, seems to be required.

We live in a multimodal society that makes its meanings by the combined use of semiotic resources, but we often make poor use of, and all too often take for granted, the increasing powers we have to create multimodal texts. Compared with previous societies, the technology we have available to us allows us to compress meaning into fewer and fewer pages and fewer and fewer visual frames.[17] Despite the persistence of common misconceptions about the way we make meanings, such as the layman's belief that 'body language' is somehow part of language and the more scholarly but still reductive 'paralinguistic' tradition which views non-linguistic resources as features tacked on to language, we are thankfully beginning to appreciate that language is just one among many meaning-making resources, perhaps more important than others but of little or no use without them.[18] We are, also, at last, witnessing the beginnings of a paradigm shift in the way language is theorized. Frameworks are thus being developed which, rather than viewing language as a single isolated semiotic resource, take into account the use of other meaning-making resources with which language is co-deployed (images, gesture, movement, voice quality, and so on).[19]

Part of this paradigm shift includes the ways in which we conceive of, and access, textual data. Within the field of translation, subtitling is a good example of this, a matter reflected in the questions we are now beginning to raise about subtitles: how will they change as society changes? how will we access them in the future? will new initiatives, such as the 'New Information Technologies' project that we mentioned at the outset, lead to subtitles being conceived as being more fully integrated into films, merging with them thanks to changes in the relationships between their linguistic and non-linguistic components (font, colour, size, type, position, movement, etc.). Or will subtitles, on the contrary, actually become more detachable from their micro-context and increasingly become managed via database storage and retrieval techniques?

This is not the place to give answers to these questions in any detail. But certainly, thanks to new technologies, we can expect a greater use of subtitling in general. With the advent of DVD and digital TV with their multiple language tracks, film media are being diffused under a translation model which, for financial reasons, relies essentially on dubbing for major languages and subtitling for minority languages.[20] Perhaps even more importantly, we can also expect new technologies to bring about changes in the way we engage with text through subtitles and hence more generally in the functions society attributes to subtitling. This paper has, for example, suggested that changes, in the way subtitles are displayed and accessed will be a first consequence of new computer technologies. As Gottlieb has pointed out:

> with digital TV just around the corner, an array of different subtitle versions could be transmitted simultaneously. In this way, slow and laidback viewers could select a subtitle option pretty much like the one they are used to, while fast and curious readers could go for a more complete version, with hardly any loss of semantic and stylistic information in the subtitles.[21]

We can thus conceive of new relationships between subtitle, source text, and the process of translating the source text, suggesting, in keeping with Gottlieb's remarks, and as we have pointed out above, that a variable, customized relationship between subtitle and viewer/reader is likely to emerge. In this respect, when considering changes in form and function in subtitling – which are perhaps more frequent than we might expect – we should recall that with the arrival of the talkies at the end of the silent movie era, the term 'subtitle' shifted its meaning from what is now expressed through the term 'intertitle' to its current meaning. The arrival of computer graphics, sound management systems that give greater control over the way L1 and L2 soundtracks are related, and the emergence of complex multimodal database retrieval systems (of which *MCA* is only a forerunner), make it legitimate to ask whether a further realignment in subtitling terminology will take place. Will it be one that will give currency to expressions such as 'language-learning subtitling', 'computerized subtitling', 'customized subtitling', and, of course, 'multimodal subtitling'? Perhaps only time will tell whether the principle of the multimodal organization of texts will take us a step further down the road in which subtitles are no longer construed as strips of language 'taped' onto a sequence of frames but rather as complex co-contextualizing texts whose incorporation within a film text needs to be carefully reconstructed within a multimodal theory of text.

NOTES

1 See S. Blane, 'Interlingual Subtitling in the Languages Degree', in *Teaching Translation in Universities: Present and Future Perspectives*, ed. P. Sewell, and I. Higgins (London: Association for French Language Studies in association with the Centre for Information on Language Teaching and Research, 1996), pp. 183–208 (p. 183).

2 S. Blane, 'Interlingual Subtitling in the Languages Degree', pp. 183–87. Throughout this paper the terms 'text' and 'film text' are based on M. A. K. Halliday's interpretation of text: 'We can define text, in the simplest way perhaps, by saying that it is language that is functional. By functional, we simply mean language that is doing some job in some context [...] So any instance of living language that is playing some part in a context of situation, we shall call text. It may be either spoken or written, or indeed in any other medium of expression that we like to think of', see M. A. K. Halliday, 'Part A', in *Language, Context and Text: Aspects of Language in a Social-semiotic Perspective*, ed. M. A. K. Halliday and R. Hasan (Oxford: Oxford University Press, 1989), pp. 1–49 (p. 10). However the terms 'text' and 'film text' are to be taken in this paper as referring to the notion of multimodal text, for which see G. Kress and Th. Van Leeuwen, *Reading Images. The Grammar of Visual Design* (London-New York: Routledge, 1996), M. O'Toole, *The Language of Displayed Art* (London: Leicester University Press, 1994), P. Thibault, 'The Multimodal Transcription of a Television Advertisement: Theory and Practice', in *Multimodality and Multimediality in the Distance-Learning Age*, ed. A. P. Baldry (Campobasso: Palladino Editore, 2000), pp. 311–85, and A. P. Baldry, 'English in a Visual Society: Historical Dimensions in Multimodality and Multimediality', in *Multimodality and Multimediality*, pp. 41–89 (pp. 65–87). It might be summarized as a conception of text as the result of the co-deployment of many meaning-making resources of which language is only one component with no preordained superior role. This view does not subscribe to the tradition that considers 'other resources such as gesture, phonological prosodies, gaze, movement and so on as paralinguistic' but instead sees them 'as fully-fledged semiotic resources in their own right with which language is co-deployed' (Thibault, 'The Multimodal Transcription of a Television Advertisement', pp. 311–12).

3 The choice of language and text was dictated by personal interest and the belief that reference to a well-known film text would facilitate the process of writing and reading the paper. The status of Italian as a minority/majority European language is not an issue discussed in this paper. Various aspects of the film, such as Benigni's highly idiolectal use of

the Tuscan variety of Italian, suggest, however, that the issue is rather more complex than it might at first appear to be.

4 C. Taylor, 'The Subtitling of Film; Reaching another Community', in *Discourse and Community: Doing Functional Linguistics*, ed. E. Ventola (Tübingen: Gunter Narr Verlag, 2000), pp. 309–27 (pp. 320–21).

5 Compared with subtitling for entertainment, the overlays in subtitling for language learning contain a substantially greater amount of information than could possibly be taken in with a single viewing. The basic constraint facing professional subtitlers, namely the need for concision, can be relaxed because the model proposed envisages multiple viewings of a particular sequence, each containing progressively more complex amounts of information, stimulating the learner to engage more profoundly with the text at each viewing. Even so, many typical recommendations (that 1-line subtitles should ideally take up 2 seconds, and 2-line subtitles 4 seconds, etc.) have (in general) been respected.

6 For the idea of 'multimodal transcription', see the following: Thibault, 'The Multimodal Transcription of a Television Advertisement', p. 311–85; A. P. Baldry, 'Introduction', in *Multimodality and Multimediality*, pp. 11–39 (pp. 28–37); Baldry, 'English in a Visual Society', pp. 68–69 and pp. 78–79; and C. Taylor and A. P. Baldry, 'Computer-assisted Text Analysis and Translation: a Functional Approach in the Analysis and Translation of Advertising Texts' in *Exploring Translation and Multilingual Text Production: Beyond Content,* eds E. Steiner and C. Yallop (Berlin: Mouton de Gruyter, 2001), pp. 277–305.

7 See Thibault, 'The Multimodal Transcription of a Television Advertisement', p. 328

8 The transcription preserves the subtitling convention of a dash to indicate a change in speaker. Except where otherwise indicated, the speaker throughout this scene is Guido Orefice *aka* Prince Guido.

9 See I. Kovačič, 'Subtitling Strategies: A Flexible Hierarchy of Priorities', in *Traduzione multimediale per il cinema, la televisione e la scena*, eds C. Heiss and R. M. Bollettieri Bosinelli (Bologna: Cooperativa Libraria Universitaria Editrice, 1996), pp. 297–305 (p. 297 and p. 302) and Taylor, 'The Subtitling of Film; Reaching another Community', p. 321. For the distinction between the ideational, interpersonal, and textual metafunctions, see M. A. K. Halliday, *An Introduction to Functional Grammar*, 2nd edn (London-Melbourne: Edward Arnold, 1994), pp. 38–144.

10 The subtitling, captioning, and intertitling procedures in this paper are well within the compass of existing widely-available postproduction tools (e.g. *Adobe Premiere*).

11 See J. Sinclair, *Corpus, Concordance, Collocation* (Oxford-Singapore: Oxford University Press, 1991), pp. 110–11.

12 See Baldry, 'Introduction', pp. 23–28; Baldry, 'English in a Visual Society', pp. 66–67 and p. 81, and Thibault, 'The Multimodal Transcription of a Television Advertisement', p. 311 and pp. 319–25.

13 See Sinclair, *Corpus, Concordance, Collocation.*

14 *MCA* is based on Windows 2000 Server and Windows Sequel Server and on the principle of query-based streaming video. It is viewable at http://eta.unipv.it/author. Details of the *Citatel* and *Linguatel* projects can be found at http://claweb.cla.unipd.it/citatal/ and http://claweb.cla.unipd.it/linguatel/.

15 See Baldry, 'English in a Visual Society', pp. 81–85, and D. Poggi, 'Design Features of Visual Databases and Corpora: Integrating Microsoft Access' (Pavia: Unpublished report for the *ACADI/CITATAL* Project: University of Pavia, 1999).

16 See M. Pavesi and A. P. Baldry 'Learning to Read Scientific Texts: Integrated Self-access Courseware and Corpora for University Science Students', in *Multimodality and Multimediality*, pp. 227–45 (p. 236).

17 See Baldry, 'Introduction', p. 11.

18 See Thibault, p. 312 and Baldry, 'Introduction', p. 15 on this principle in relation to turn-taking.

19 See Baldry, 'Introduction', p. 11 and Thibault, p. 312.

20 See H. Gottlieb, *Screen Translation 2000: Six Studies in Subtitling, Dubbing and Voice-over* (Copenhagen: Center for Translation Studies, Department of English, University of Copenhagen, 2000), p. 34.

21 See Gottlieb, *Screen Translation 2000*, p. 20.

RELEVANCE THEORY AND SIMULTANEOUS INTERPRETING: IMPLICATIONS FOR TEACHING

Annalisa Sandrelli
University of Hull

Relevance theory is a communication theory developed by Dan Sperber and Deirdre Wilson in the 1980s as an alternative to 'code model' based theories.[1] The latter, which basically argue that speakers encode messages by selecting and combining signs, then decoded by hearers, overlook the central issue of communication, namely that the linguistic meaning of a sentence (and the corresponding semantic representation) does not always coincide with the overall meaning of an utterance. The hearer must further process the semantic representation to complete it with *inferences* drawn from the *context*.[2] The full meaning intended by the speaker is a propositional form. In the words of Sperber and Wilson, 'there is a gap between the semantic representations of sentences and the thoughts actually communicated by utterances. The gap is filled not by mere coding but by inference'.[3]

The *context*, formed by the premises used by the hearer to interpret an utterance, does not refer to the physical environment in which the act of communication takes place, but to 'a psychological construct, a subset of the hearer's assumptions about the world'.[4] Each new utterance is interpreted in a new context, which incorporates the previous utterance. In this sense, context includes not only the hearer's encyclopaedic knowledge and knowledge of the speaker, but also knowledge accumulated during the act of communication itself, namely the *co-text*.

The speaker expects the hearer to draw inferences from the intended context: this implies that for communication to be successful speakers and hearers must share the context, that is, there must be a *mutual cognitive environment.* The code model does not explain how speakers and hearers distinguish the assumptions they share from those they do not share. According to this model, hearers and speakers are forced to make second-order assumptions about the first-order assumptions they may share; however, in order to make sure they share these second-order assumptions, they have to make third-order assumptions, and so on. Clearly, the process can go on infinitely, in an attempt to establish *mutual knowledge.*[5] Sperber and Wilson reject the mutual knowledge hypothesis and the code model on which it is based. They attempt to provide a solution to the problem with the concept of *relevance.*

In this paper, I aim to show that Relevance Theory (RT) can provide the theoretical tools which students of interpreting need to analyse practice texts (speeches) and their Target Language (TL) interpretations of them.

Sperber and Wilson make a distinction between *primary communication situations* and *secondary communication situations.* The former term describes those situations in which the hearer uses the speaker-intended contextual assumptions in processing a message, so that communication can be defined as successful. The latter indicates all those situations in which, for whatever reason, the hearer does not use the speaker-intended context, often resulting in misinterpretation. Therefore, the basic problem of communication is: how does the hearer distinguish speaker-intended assumptions from other assumptions?

RT argues that the main criterion used by speakers and hearers is *relevance.*[6] The goal of human cognition is to increase the quantity and improve the quality and structure of an individual's knowledge: 'To achieve this goal as efficiently as possible, the individual must at each moment try to allocate his processing resources to the most *relevant* information: that is [...] information likely to bring about the greatest improvement of knowledge at the smallest processing cost'.[7] Basically, the hearer expects the necessary contextual assumptions to be easily accessible, so that the effort needed to retrieve them is small. Moreover, the hearer also expects the processing effort to produce some benefits, namely a worthwhile modification of his own contextual assumptions. Such modifications are referred to as *contextual effects.* When processing an utterance, the accessibility of information in our minds is correlated with the effort required to recall it. This means that 'other things being equal, an assumption with greater contextual effects is more relevant; and, other things being equal, an assumption requiring a smaller processing effort is more relevant'.[8] Consequently, the hearer will accept the first interpretation of the utterance which is consistent with the principle of relevance as the speaker-intended interpretation. This implies that in RT the notion of context is not *given* but *chosen* by the hearer. The hearer chooses the context on the basis of its accessibility (i.e. low processing effort) and on the basis of the potential contextual effects which can be derived from it. Sperber and Wilson note that 'people hope that the assumption being processed is relevant [...] and they try to select a context which will justify that hope: a context which will maximise relevance. In verbal comprehension in particular, it is relevance that is treated as given and context which is treated as variable'.[9]

Clearly, the principle of optimal relevance applies to the speaker as well, i.e. in order to achieve optimal relevance, he should try to formulate his speech in such a way that the first interpretation likely to occur to the hearer is the one intended.[10] For example, the speaker must be aware that 'encyclopaedic knowledge [...] makes certain assumptions highly accessible; if these lead on to interpretations consistent with the principle of relevance, all other lines of interpretation are disallowed'.[11]

The above does not mean that the speaker must always say exactly what he thinks, i.e. use *descriptive language* all the time. Language can be used *interpretively* too. For example, a speaker can utter 'This bag weighs a ton' without anybody believing that the bag actually weighs a ton. The hearers' encyclopaedic knowledge tells them that a person cannot lift one thousand kilos and that bags do not weigh a ton. On the basis of this, the literal interpretation is discarded and hearers arrive at the speaker's intended interpretation, which is 'This bag is very heavy'. The utterance is not interpreted as a description of a state of affairs, but as an utterance which interpretively resembles another one. In both descriptive and interpretive language use, context plays an important role in sentence disambiguation. In particular, it enables hearers to distinguish *explicatures* (that is, propositional forms to be interpreted literally) from *implicatures* (instances of metaphorical language).[12]

From the above, it follows that the use of the wrong context may result in misinterpretations. The importance attributed to context in RT is what prompted Ernst August Gutt to apply the RT framework to translation.[13] Gutt criticizes the necessity of a 'translation theory', and claims that translation can be seen as a special case within the RT framework. More specifically, Gutt argues that translation can be considered as *interlingual interpretive use of language*.[14] It is easy to see that translation may often fall within the secondary communication situation category, since the translator does not always have access to the context intended by the producer of the source language (SL) text, owing to the passing of time, or to cultural differences. Moreover, the

TL audience does not always have access to the text-producer's intended context.

According to RT, in order to communicate the same interpretation intended in the original, a translation must 'convey to the receptors *all and only those explicatures and implicatures that the original was intended to convey*'.[15] However, it is seldom possible to convey the same explicatures and implicatures as the original in a different language, without adding some which were not intended by the speaker and/or without losing some which were intended. This is due not only to the differences between the two languages involved, but also to the cultural differences between the original audience and the TL audience. Therefore, a weaker reading of the above rule is: 'The sum total of the explicatures and implicatures of the translation must equal the sum total of the explicatures and implicatures of the original'.[16] In other words, a translation should interpretively resemble the original only in those respects which make it adequately relevant to the TL audience.[17] In this sense, faithfulness to the original can take different forms, depending on the context in which the translation is going to be interpreted.[18]

One of the consequences of the above notion of translation is that the success (or otherwise) of a translation depends not only on what is expressed in the text, but also on the contextual knowledge of the TL audience. In Gutt's words 'a translation can communicate the full intended meaning of the original only if the receptor audience has access to the full context envisaged by the original communicator'.[19]

Gutt's arguments for considering translation as a special case within the general framework of RT refer mainly to written translation. However, there is no reason why his arguments may not apply to SI as well: indeed he does make a few references to interpreting, although they are not central to his argument.

The situation of the conference interpreter is even more complex than that of the translator. Although the problems of context apply to interpreting as well, the speaker, the audience, and the interpreter share the physical context in which communication is taking place, i.e. the conference. As Robin Setton, who has applied RT to the analysis of a large corpus of interpreted speeches, points out, 'the interpreter therefore has both more and less relevant context than the translator, and both more and fewer resources: for comprehension, she has perceptual access to the event, intonational clues, and sometimes, immediate feedback from Addressees; and for expression, the resource of intonation'.[20]

In one of his passing references to conference interpreting, Gutt claims that the 'rules' for good interpreting found in the literature can be seen as applications of RT to this type of translation. For example, discussing Namy's advice to interpreters that they should take liberties with the original if that makes the message clearer, Gutt explains that 'from the relevance-theoretic point of view this guideline is motivated by the fact that the translation will be taken up aurally. Since the stream of speech flows on, the audience cannot be expected to sit and ponder difficult renderings [...]; hence it needs to be able to recover the intended meaning instantly'.[21]

This comment highlights the main difference between translation and interpreting, namely the *time factor*. Firstly, the time factor may influence the speaker's choices in terms of style and content. Since the audience will only hear the speech once, and is not usually given a written copy, the speaker must strive to produce a speech which is as comprehensible and effective as possible. In particular, he may wish to use certain pragmatic devices to guide the audience to the relevant contexts needed to arrive at the intended meanings.[22] Secondly, the audience has to recover the meanings intended by the speaker using the correct contexts. However, audiences at multilingual conferences always include some people who understand the speaker's language, and others who rely on the interpreting service. Can optimal relevance be achieved for all of them? Lastly, the time factor influences the interpreter's translation choices, since 'given the requirement of divided attention and immediacy of response, the simultaneous interpreter concentrates on processing only current input'.[23] The interpreter exploits various sources of information to succeed in the task. Professional interpreters have developed high sensitivity to the linguistic 'signposts' chosen by the speaker to guide the audience to the intended context.[24]

Another complicating factor is the special status of the interpreter in the communicative situation. Unlike the translator, she is at once speaker and hearer. The interpreter listens to the speaker, but she is not directly addressed by the speaker. Moreover, she does not listen out of personal interest, but in order to translate what is being said for that part of the intended audience which does not understand the SL. The simultaneous interpreter does not interact with the speaker or the audience, in fact, she is physically isolated from them (in the booth) and her presence is not always acknowledged by all the participants.[25] In other words, the interpreter is not a primary addressee, but rather a *ratified overhearer*.[26]

The special status of the interpreter has a number of practical consequences. The interpreter takes for granted that the speaker has a message for the audience, and that the audience will be in a position to retrieve the speaker-intended context. However, the interpreter does not necessarily share the contextual assumptions of the speaker and the audience. According to the principle of relevance, this means that the processing effort required to identify the correct context is likely to be higher for the interpreter. This is why so much importance is attached to preparation before a professional assignment. The interpreter must try to build, in the short time available before the job, the necessary knowledge (of the topic, of the speaker, of the audience, of the aim of the meeting, etc.). This information enables the interpreter to anticipate the development of the speech. In his analysis of a corpus of interpreted speeches, Setton found numerous examples of *anticipation*, i.e. cases in which the interpreter 'translated' something before it was actually uttered by the speaker. Whilst interpreting, the interpreter creates a *mental model* of the speech which is constantly updated as new information is processed. Every new utterance is processed and checked against the mental model, to see if it is compatible. Clearly, the overriding principle is one of relevance: 'a simultaneous interpreter (having no access to the speaker's sentence plan) relies strongly on clues to the logical direction of the discourse, and specifically, on the relative weight or significance which the speaker intends to attach to the information he presents and evokes, and how he intends it to be processed'.[27]

Textual and extratextual sources enable the interpreter to make approximations and generalizations, on the basis of which she can say something plausible in the context of what the speaker has said up to that point. Evidence from Setton's corpus suggests that 'a small number of conceptual complexes [...] are highly accessible to the process of assembling propositional forms for production, so that the interpreter can, if necessary, safely produce relevant or at least uncontroversial assertions of qualifications about them when they are instantiated in the text'.[28]

It is possible to gloss a number of teaching precepts commonly used in interpreter training institutions in terms of RT. For example, one of the basic 'rules' says that you must never leave a sentence unfinished, even if you have missed one part of it. Clearly, this is possible only if the interpreter uses her mental model to produce something relevant or at least neutral. Indeed, another important rule tells students to adopt the policy of least commitment if in doubt about the meaning of a sentence, i.e. produce a vague utterance which can be easily corrected or to which information can be added later on. Once again, in relevance-theoretic terms this rule would imply using the mental model to produce a sentence that is likely to have adequate contextual effects, even if its interpretive resemblance to the original is not as high as it could have been.

Even interpreting 'strategies', which are applied by interpreters to save time and produce a more fluent, better-structured TL rendition, can be seen as an application of the principle of relevance. Let us take the so-called *salami technique*, which suggests dividing long, cumbersome sentences into several short, self-contained utterances.[29] Conference speeches often belong to the hybrid category of texts written to be read aloud. While certain structures pose no particular processing problem to a reader, they may be extremely difficult for an audience which only receives the message orally. Streamlining the original is advisable in simultaneous interpreting because it makes comprehension easier for the audience, i.e. it makes the TL version more relevant to the audience. Another suggestion to trainee interpreters is to maximize efficiency by avoiding repetitions, discarding filler words and rhetorical expressions, and so forth. It is easy to see why: all of the above are irrelevant, i.e. the effort required to process them does not bring about worthwhile contextual effects.

Over the last twenty years the literature on interpreting, and specifically on interpreter training, has been developing steadily. As a result, there are now several handbooks, manuals, and articles dealing with pedagogic issues.[30] Most of these publications describe the exercises which students can do in class and in their own time to improve their interpreting skills. They also describe real-life professional challenges and give advice on how to tackle them. Most importantly, such handbooks suggest strategies and rules which student interpreters are to follow in their training and in their professional lives. Gutt acknowledges that, in the related field of (written) translation, rules and guidelines collected by professional translators can be very useful to other translators.[31] Clearly, the same can be said of the literature on interpreter training, since it is based on the professional and pedagogic experience of interpreter trainers, almost always interpreters themselves.

It is my firm belief, however, that student interpreters would greatly benefit from being exposed to the basic concepts of RT during their training. By applying the principles of RT to the analysis of their work, students gain a deeper, less intuitive understanding of the nature of their craft. This enables them to tackle new difficulties with the same ease as those for which established routines exist. RT can be useful on two levels. Firstly, it can enhance the interpreter's comprehension of the SL text. In particular, RT highlights the difference between linguistic expression and speaker-intended interpretation, which, as was seen above, is a key issue in translation and interpreting. Secondly, knowledge of RT enhances the important role of contextual information. RT helps the interpreter understand the original context, and makes her aware of its accessibility (or otherwise) to the TL audience. This includes an appreciation of cultural differences which may make it necessary to render information explicit to the TL audience. It also means researching what the audience expects of the interpretation, in other words, finding out what use the audience will make of the TL text. As Gutt says, 'The particular interests of the target audience, whether, for example, they have "literary interests" or simply want information, are another important part of the contextual background'.[32] Since students do not have an audience during classes (apart from the teacher), they tend to forget that the interpretation is a text which is meant for immediate 'consumption' by the audience.[33] This is one of the reasons why classroom practice should be supplemented by 'mock conferences' or by practising in a mute booth in a real conference. A deeper understanding of what the communication process involves enables trainees to produce a better interpretation, i.e. an interpretation that offers worthwhile contextual effects to the audience.

So, when interpreting, students should constantly be asking themselves: 'what is likely to bring about the best contextual effects for my audience?' In the following I will present a practical application. The speech chosen as an example is the address by Queen Elizabeth II at the banquet offered by the President of Italy during Her Majesty's State Visit on 16 October 2000 (see Appendix for full text).

The Queen's speech came in response to President Ciampi's toast. Toasts can be seen as a sub-genre within the genre of political speeches. In our case the speakers are two Heads of State, which narrows down the scope of such speeches even further: State Visits are meticulously planned and nothing is left to improvisation, including, of course, speeches. The speakers are performing official duties and therefore are not speaking for themselves, but rather as representatives of their nations. As noted by T. Ensink, this results in 'the eclipse of the individuality of the speaker'.[34] In their representative functions, Heads of State are not expected to express personal opinions. In particular, speeches delivered during state visits normally serve the purpose of strengthening the relationship between two countries.

Clearly, this is an advantage for the interpreter (professional or student) who can expect a high degree of predictability and anticipate the contents of the speeches more easily. Generally speaking, toasts delivered by Heads of State have the following structure: introduction and thanks; first part, in which the historical ties between the two countries are mentioned; second part, in which the present ties (economic, political, social) between the two countries are examined and reference is made to future developments; conclusion (including the toast).

Since this event is not a conference, the audience is untypical as well: it includes the Queen's party, the President's staff, a few guests of honour, journalists, and, although not physically present, the peoples of both countries, represented by their Heads of State.[35]

In addition to researching the composition of the audience, the interpreter must also find out about the background of the speakers. In this case, any Italian interpreter with English as a passive language can be expected to know 'quite a lot' about a public figure like the Queen. On the other hand, an English-speaking interpreter interpreting President Ciampi's speech would be well-advised to try to find out about his education and career as an economist and as a politician.[36]

A simple exercise that can be performed in class is to ask student interpreters to try to predict the content of a speech on the basis of what they know about the situation and the speakers. In our case, we can be certain that the Queen will start her speech by thanking her host. This is not her first State Visit to Italy, so we can imagine that reference will be made to her past visits. Bearing in mind that the speech was delivered in the year 2000, an informed student interpreter would expect some reference to the Millennium or the Catholic Jubilee, both of them very much in the news throughout that year. Then, following the typical structure of toasts, a brief mention of the historical ties between Italy and Britain can be expected. However, the Queen's aim in her speech is certainly to talk about the present and the future, rather than the past. Therefore, the speech will almost certainly dwell on the present relationship between the two countries. In terms of politics, both countries are part of the EU, NATO, and G8: they have, therefore, a lot in common, particularly in the fields of foreign affairs and defence. In this regard, a good knowledge of current affairs would prompt the interpreter to expect some reference to the involvement of both countries in the peace-keeping operations in the Balkans. Moreover, the Queen is likely to talk about developing the already strong economic relationship between the UK and Italy.

The above is an example of how to build a mental model of the interpreting assignment before the latter actually starts. The contents of the model will be modified as the speaker goes along, but it is extremely important to have the background picture ready in one's mind before the speech begins. Comprehension is made easier and anticipation becomes possible, thus saving processing resources for the unforeseeable parts of the speech, in which the speaker displays his (in our case, her) creativity.

Let us begin to analyse the speech and see how RT can help students in processing. As expected, the speech is rather neatly divided into introduction (sections 1–3); first part, recalling the historical ties between the two countries (4–7); second part, describing the current political and economic ties (8–13); and conclusion (14–15). Within these large sections, smaller portions, roughly corresponding to paragraphs, can be identified. The structure of the text is carefully built: connectives such as 'but', 'and', 'yet', and 'so' are used to mark the beginning of new paragraphs, thus strengthening the overall cohesion of the text. Even at a cursory glance, it is evident that the speech belongs to the text type 'written to be read aloud'.

Throughout the speech, the Queen makes reference to the situational context through deictics (indexicals and demonstratives), such as 'your city' (2), 'the north of your country' (3), 'your country' and 'your land' (4), 'here' (4), 'today', 'now' (5), 'these days', 'tomorrow' (6), and so forth. The contextual information needed to interpret these elements is easily accessible: however, the interpreter must bear in mind the needs of the audience. Therefore, she has to choose whether to translate 'your' with 'la sua, il suo, etc.' (that is, referring to President Ciampi) or with 'la vostra, il vostro, etc.' (referring to the Italian people).

Another textual element which reveals careful preparation and the essentially written nature of the speech is the use of both anaphora and cataphora.[37] Examples of anaphora are: 'a few on the Grand Tour [...] *those early visitors*' (5), 'the Alps and the Channel, *those two great natural frontiers*' (6), 'our young people [...] *Theirs*' (7), 'two very different nations, *the one* Atlantic and *the other* Mediterranean' (8), 'freedom, and *with it*' (8), 'countries [...] *For those*' (8–9), 'the people in the Balkans. For many *of them*' (10), and 'all the states of former Yugoslavia [...] *that troubled region*' (10–11). Examples of cataphora are: '*on this* my third State Visit' (2), throughout *its* long history [...] your country (4), and 'Through *its* achievements, *its* inventions, *its* culture and *its* way of life, Italy' (4).

The Queen starts her speech by acknowledging the presence of her hosts and of the audience, with a clear reference to the situational context ('Mr President, Ladies and Gentlemen'). Then, in the first paragraph, she gives the customary thanks to her host: this is a form of feedback, because the Queen makes reference to the previous speech made by President Ciampi ('for your kind words of welcome'). Then comes the expected mention of the previous State Visits made by the Queen and Prince Philip.

The second paragraph presents few unexpected elements in terms of coherence with the mental model, but poses a translation problem, namely the mention of the Millennium year and the Jubilee. To an English-speaking audience, the word 'Millennium' poses no comprehension problems: the context for interpreting it correctly (i.e. as the year 2000) is highly accessible. The word has some religious overtones, but it is not used exclusively in a religious sense. On the other hand, in Italy the same year is most commonly called the 'Jubilee'. The Italian word 'giubileo' is used to refer to a particular Catholic anniversary:

'nella chiesa cattolica, periodo, che generalmente ricorre ogni 25 anni e ha durata annuale, in cui il Pontefice concede l'indulgenza plenaria ai fedeli che si rechino pellegrini a Roma o che compiano opere meritorie equivalenti'.[38] The year 2000 was particularly important for the Catholic church, because it was a jubilee year that also marked two millennia since the birth of Christ. However, in British English, the word jubilee is used to refer to an anniversary, often in connection with the Monarchy. Clearly, in this case the Queen uses 'jubilee' in the Catholic sense of the word. Therefore, the translation of this particular item into Italian poses no particular problem, as long as the interpreter understands what the Queen means. On the other hand, when translating 'Millennium' into Italian the interpreter must be aware of the fact that 'millennio' may not be sufficient to make the relevant context accessible to the audience. Therefore, she will add a word of explanation, such as 'quest'anno, che segna l'inizio del terzo millennio'.

In paragraph 2, the Queen makes explicit reference to the improved appearance of the city of Rome, after the extensive restoration works carried out for the Jubilee. This contextual information should be easily accessible to a student interpreter who keeps up-to-date and reads the papers. Therefore this paragraph should not pose particular translation problems. Paragraph 3 is also better understood if the background information is clear in the interpreter's mind, namely that both Italy and the United Kingdom suffered extensive floods in September and October 2000. Once again, the interpreter can be expected to know about it.

Paragraph 4 marks the end of the introductory remarks and the beginning of the actual speech. In order to interpret this part of the speech correctly, the interpreter will have to draw on her encyclopaedic knowledge, and in particular on knowledge of history of the two countries. The reference to 'generations of British travellers' should immediately trigger the concept of the Grand Tour in the interpreter's mind. By adding this concept to the mental model, when the explicit reference to the Grand Tour actually comes in paragraph 5, the interpreter is not caught off her guard. Then, the interpreter realizes that the speaker-intended context is not necessarily shared by the Italian-speaking audience and that some explanation of 'Grand Tour' is required.

This historical sweep is then followed by three paragraphs (5, 6, and 7) describing the current state of the relationship between the British and Italian peoples, focusing on tourism, the media, sport, and education. In paragraph 6 there is an allusion to movements of people between the two countries, namely Italian immigration to the United Kingdom (and to Scotland in particular) and the large numbers of British expatriates who have settled in Tuscany (the so-called

'Chiantishire'). Once again, the interpreter's encyclopaedic knowledge comes in handy to correctly identify the speaker's intended meaning.

Paragraph 8 marks the beginning of the second part of the speech, in which the Queen addresses the really important issues of political and economic relations between Italy and the United Kingdom. The interpreter expects a mention of the EU, NATO, and G8, of which both Italy and the UK are members. However, the sentence 'We are two very different nations – the one Atlantic and the other Mediterranean' comes as an unexpected shift in the direction of what divides Italy and the UK. Balance is restored in the following sentence, which once again stresses that the two countries have a good deal in common. The presence of the connective 'yet' must trigger the speaker's intended meaning in the interpreter's mind. The mental model tells her that Italy and the UK enjoy a close political relationship, and her encyclopaedic knowledge also tells her that the aim of the Queen's speech must surely be to foster it even further. Therefore, she will correctly identify the above-mentioned structures as a rhetorical device, setting up a contrast between the two countries, only to reaffirm their closeness.

The concluding sentences in this paragraph are based on a very careful parallel construction, highlighting the contrast between the peace and economic prosperity enjoyed by the countries in Western Europe (and note that in this case the pronoun 'we' does not refer to the United Kingdom only), and the long years of dictatorship endured by the countries of Eastern Europe ('them').

Paragraph 9 is very short, but plays an important role in the structure of this part of the speech. It starts with a strong anaphoric link to the previous sentence ('for those' refers back to 'countries in Eastern Europe'), which the interpreter must notice and use to retain textual cohesion in the TL version. What this paragraph actually means is that the United Kingdom is prepared to accept few new members into the European Union for now, i.e. only 'those whose economies and institutions are prepared for it'. The interpreter can arrive at the correct interpretation if she bears in mind that the UK is one of the least enthusiastic members of the EU on the issue of enlargement. However, the interpreter must also note the very careful wording used by the Queen, and must produce an equally diplomatic TL version.

Paragraphs 10 and 11 dwell on the situation in the Balkans and on the involvement of Italy and the UK there, through participation in KFOR. The only potential difficulty in these two paragraphs is the correct identification of the referents of the personal pronouns. For example, in the first sentence in paragraph 10 the pronoun 'us' could refer to either the United Kingdom or the United Kingdom and Italy, or Western Europe. In this case the freshly updated mental model should assist the interpreter in deciding to treat it as an anaphoric reference to 'the United Kingdom' of the previous sentence. In these two paragraphs, anaphoric devices are extensively used: the opening 'this' at the beginning of paragraph 11 refers to the entire paragraph 10, while 'that troubled region' has a clearly identifiable antecedent in 'the states of former Yugoslavia'. In both cases, the interpreter can exploit these devices in the TL version as well.

In paragraph 11 there is again a change in the referents of 'we' and 'you'. Whilst in the previous paragraph 'we' meant both Italy and the UK, in paragraph 11 'you' ('you have worked tirelessly') definitely refers to Italy only. However, later in the same paragraph, the adjective 'our' ('our armed forces') once again includes both countries. While these shifts in meaning may seem very easy to understand when analysing the written speech, they are decidedly more difficult to pick up in a simultaneous interpreting condition, in which the interpreter has only a few seconds to react. It is the use of the mental model that helps the interpreter choose the correct context and arrive at the correct interpretation. Among the different possible interpretations which spring to mind, the interpreter will choose the most relevant one, the one that fits in more coherently with the mental model of the speech which she has been elaborating thus far.

Paragraphs 12 and 13 are much more straightforward than the previous ones, in that there is no ambiguity as to the meaning of the pronoun 'we', which always refers to both countries here. The Queen is talking about the commercial relations between them, and the only detail to which the students' attention could be drawn is the mention of the Queen's planned visit to Milan. On the day, the official interpreter was certainly given the programme of the State Visit, so she must have known that the Queen was going to Milan after Rome.

Finally, the last two paragraphs make up the conclusion of the Queen's speech. The first one sums up the various themes discussed in the speech, namely the past, the present, and the future of the relationship between Italy and the UK. The interpreter can effortlessly anticipate this, since, as we know, it matches the typical structure of toasts. The Queen addresses President Ciampi directly, as she did in the opening remarks. Moreover, she begins the first sentence of paragraph 14 with the phrase 'it gives me special pleasure', which is a clear signal that she is about to wind down the speech. The interpreter must react and activate the standard TL expressions for closing speeches. These are parts of the discourse which the interpreter does not really need to process, and it is therefore advisable to memorize them.

This kind of exercise, which applies the principles of RT to interpreting in the classroom, trains students to pay attention to certain aspects of the text and to matters of context which in a high-pressure simultaneous interpreting condition may easily escape them. In a way, this type of analysis is a slow rehearsal of the thought processes which take place in interpreting the same text. Although instinct may sometimes guide students to the correct interpretation, it is useful to draw their attention to certain aspects of the communicative situation, so that the next time they are faced with a similar difficulty, they know how to deal with it. Indeed, the application of RT to the teaching of interpreting does not result in a number of normative rules for students to follow. On the contrary, by its very nature RT is very general. Its biggest contribution to the teaching of interpreting is that it gives students the tools to understand the issues at stake in interpreting any given utterance for any given audience. Too often students in the booth forget that they are meant to be speaking to an audience, and that the TL version must be comprehensible. By moving the focus away from the text and onto the communicative situation (onto the possible mismatch between the context used by the speaker and the needs of the audience in particular), the application of RT to the teaching of interpreting can fill a gap in existing pedagogical methods.

APPENDIX: Speech given by The Queen at the State Banquet (Quirinale Palace, Rome, 16 October 2000)

Mr President, Ladies and Gentlemen

(1) May I start by thanking you, Mr President, for your kind words of welcome. It is the greatest pleasure for both Prince Philip and me to return to Italy. We first came here nearly fifty years ago in 1951 from Malta, and we have the happiest memories of our previous State Visits in 1961 and 1980.

(2) On this my third State Visit it is a particular privilege to be in Rome during this Millennium year. I have already been able to see something of how splendid your city is looking for the occasion. I can only admire the vision and application of those many people who have worked to prepare for this Jubilee.

(3) May I take this opportunity to mention the torrential floods which have caused such damage in the north of your country over the weekend. Regions in both our countries have suffered badly from floods in recent days and I would like to express my heartfelt sympathy to all those in both our countries who have been affected by these disasters, including in particular the families of those who have tragically lost their lives in Northern Italy.

(4) Throughout its long history, longer by far than the two millennia which we celebrate this year, your country has had an astonishing capacity to attract and influence the rest of the world – including in particular those from my country. Through its achievements, its inventions, its culture and its way of life, Italy captivates us all in a direct and personal way. Generations of British travellers, including many members of my family, have over the years been drawn inexorably to your land to discover for themselves the creative genius here which has done so much to define western civilisation as we now know it.

(5) But happily travel to Italy is today not the preserve of a few on the Grand Tour. Millions now follow in the footsteps of those early visitors. Italy and the United Kingdom are drawn

together by an ever-expanding web of contacts and links between our two peoples.

(6) Italian and British artists and designers, bankers and entrepreneurs cross the Alps and the Channel, those two great natural frontiers, in search of inspiration in each other's cities. Local groups in Scotland and elsewhere trace their ancestry back to Italy. And these days I expect your compatriots to the north of here wonder at the thriving British communities who have discovered the paradise of Tuscany. Our singers, actors, and sports teams are household names in both Britain and Italy. Football alone brings together thousands of supporters to each other's countries, as it will tomorrow at the stadium here in Rome.

(7) And our young people do not just visit: they stay and study in each other's universities and colleges. Theirs is the future and we need to encourage in every way this vital investment, from school level onwards.

(8) With so much going on each day between our peoples, we should not be surprised at the ever-increasing co-operation at government level. We share values and we share commitments – in the European Union, in NATO and in the G8. We are two very different nations – the one Atlantic and the other Mediterranean. Yet we find so much in our rapidly changing world which makes us natural partners. In Western Europe we have now enjoyed freedom, and with it growing prosperity and security, for over half a century. Countries in Eastern Europe have emerged more recently from dictatorship and tyranny.

(9) For those whose economies and institutions are prepared for it, the European Union is a natural home. The United Kingdom is committed to ensuring that it is a home whose doors are open in welcome.

(10) Others to the East of us have had a longer struggle for freedom. The British people, like the Italian people, have been moved and outraged by the suffering of the people in the Balkans. For many of them, the collapse of communism meant not freedom but civil war, persecution, and hardship. We rejoice that the prospect is opening up for all the states of former Yugoslavia of joining the European mainstream.

(11) This has brought the United Kingdom and Italy even closer together. For Italy, that troubled region is a near neighbour. You have worked tirelessly with friends and allies to bring it stability. Britain's armed forces and civilians have been heavily engaged there too with your outstanding support. Our armed forces continue to serve alongside each other in Kosovo, and British troops are now being led by the Italian commander of the KFOR who took command today.

(12) Our defence relationship has never been stronger. So it is especially appropriate that, during my visit to Rome, I shall be able to meet British and Italian military personnel who have served together in an effort to bring to people in the Balkans the reality of the fundamental right to live in peace and security.

(13) The United Kingdom and Italy are both leading world economies and we are amongst each other's most important commercial partners. Under the impetus of globalization and new technology, the way in which we do business is changing before our eyes. We are both well placed to benefit from these trends. I look forward to my visit to Milan later this week, to see for myself how the commercial skills of our two great countries combine to strengthen us both.

(14) It gives me special pleasure, President Ciampi, to recognize that popular affection and shared interests of the present, as well as our common approaches to the future, combined always with a celebration of such a rich past, are at the heart of our relationship today. This for me is the significance of this State Visit and of these next few days in Italy.

(15) Ladies and Gentlemen, I ask you all to stand and join me in a toast to 'the President and the people of Italy'.

NOTES

1 D. Sperber and D. Wilson, 'Relevance', in *Relevance: Communication and Cognition*, 2nd edn (Cambridge-Massachusetts-Oxford: Blackwell Publishers, 1995), pp. 118–71. Following a

common convention, in this paper the terms 'speaker' and 'hearer' will be assumed to be masculine, while the term 'interpreter' will be assumed to be feminine.

2 The full meaning intended by the speaker is a *propositional form*. Indeed, the same utterance can be used to convey opposite meanings, according to the context in which it is interpreted. Gutt gives a clear example of this in E. Gutt, 'Pragmatic Aspects of Translation: Some Relevance-Theory Observations', in *The Pragmatics of Translation*, ed. L. Hickey (Clevedon–Philadelphia–Toronto–Sydney–Johannesburg: Multilingual Matters Ltd, 1998), pp 41–53. The following exchange can be interpreted in different ways (pp. 41–42):

Joe: Will Sarah be long?
Pam: She is with Frank now.

Pam's answer could mean that Sarah will be ready soon, if Frank is known for his speed in dealing with people; on the other hand, it could mean that Sarah will be busy for hours, if Frank is known for keeping people in his office for a very long time.

3 D. Sperber and D. Wilson, 'Précis of *Relevance: Communication and Cognition*', in *Readings in Language and Mind*, ed. H. Geirsson and M. Losonsky (Cambridge-Massachussetts-Oxford: Blackwell Publishers, 1996), pp. 460–86 (p. 461).

4 Sperber and Wilson, 'Précis of *Relevance: Communication and Cognition*', p. 463.

5 Sperber and Wilson, 'Précis of *Relevance: Communication and Cognition*', p. 462.

6 According to Sperber and Wilson, 'human attention and thought, [...] automatically turn toward information which seems relevant: To communicate is to claim someone's attention, hence to communicate is to imply that the information communicated is relevant', 'Précis of *Relevance: Communication and Cognition*', p. 460. In every communicative situation speakers and hearers share the assumption that what is communicated is a message worth communicating.

7 Sperber and Wilson, 'Précis of *Relevance: Communication and Cognition*', p. 465.

8 Sperber and Wilson, 'Précis of *Relevance: Communication and Cognition*', p. 470–71.

9 Sperber and Wilson, 'Précis of *Relevance: Communication and Cognition*', p. 142.

10 See D. Wilson and D. Sperber, 'Pragmatics and Time', in *Relevance Theory. Applications and Implications*, eds R. Carston and S. Uchida (Amsterdam–Philadelphia: John Benjamins Publishing Company, 1998), pp. 1–22 (pp. 10–11).

11 Wilson and Sperber, 'Pragmatics and Time', p. 15.

12 Sperber and Wilson, 'Précis of *Relevance: Communication and Cognition*', pp. 474–83.

13 E. A. Gutt, *Translation and Relevance. Cognition and Context* (Manchester: St Jerome Publishing, 2000).

14 'From the relevance-theory point of view, translation falls naturally under the interpretive use of language: the translation is intended to restate in one language what someone else said or wrote in another language', Gutt, *Translation and Relevance. Cognition and Context*, p. 46.

15 Gutt, *Translation and Relevance. Cognition and Context*, p. 99.

16 Gutt, *Translation and Relevance. Cognition and Context*, p. 100.

17 See E. A. Gutt, *Relevance Theory. A Guide to Successful Communication in Translation* (Dallas: Summer Institute of Linguistics and United Bible Societies, 1992), p. 42.

18 Gutt's example involving the translation of a German poem into English is clear (Gutt, *Relevance Theory*, pp. 42–44). A simple gloss is faithful in that it enables those readers who do not know German to find out the semantic content of the poem in order to follow the discussion on faithfulness. A translation which attempts to reproduce the formal characteristics of the text (rhyme, alliteration, etc.) is faithful, in that it enables the readers to see what the German poet was trying to do.

19 Gutt, *Relevance Theory*, p. 67.

20 R. Setton, *Simultaneous Interpretation: A Cognitive Pragmatic Analysis* (Amsterdam–Philadelphia: John Benjamins Publishing Company, 1999), p. 10.

21 Gutt, *Translation and Relevance. Cognition and Context*, p. 123.

22 Setton, *Simultaneous Interpretation*, p. 8.

23 B. Hatim and I. Mason, *The Translator as Communicator* (London: Routledge, 1997), p. 63.

24 In this sense, Basil Hatim and Ian Mason talk about the prominence of *texture* in SI. In an analysis of a number of French speeches the two authors highlight what they call 'expectation-creating signals' (p. 65), such as enumerations. They also stress the importance of

including the study of textural signals in an interpreter training programme.

25 Participants who do not need the interpreting service may not always realize that the interpreter is there.

26 In the words of Basil Hatim and Ian Mason, 'the interpreter's response will not be one of interaction with an interlocutor but rather of sympathetic impersonation of a source text speaker – with a similar group of addressees in mind to that of the speaker', Hatim and Mason, *The Translator as Communicator*, p. 63.

27 Setton, *Simultaneous Interpretation*, p. 11.

28 Setton, *Simultaneous Interpretation*, p. 192.

29 R. Jones, *Conference Interpreting Explained* (Manchester: St. Jerome Publishing, 1998), p. 101.

30 See for example the following titles: D. Seleskovitch and M. Lederer, *Pédagogie raisonnée de l'interprétation* (Paris: Didier Erudition, 1989); D. Snelling, *Strategies for Simultaneous Interpreting. From Romance Languages into English* (Udine: Campanotto Editore, 1992); and C. Falbo, M. Russo, and F. Straniero Sergio (eds), *Interpretazione simultanea e consecutiva. Problemi teorici e metodologie didattiche* (Milan: Ulrico Hoepli, 1999).

31 'In many cases these generalizations reflect what particular features or class of features are likely to be of special relevance to a particular audience. Such generalizations are very useful indeed because not every audience is completely different in all aspects from any other audience', Gutt, *Translation and Relevance*, p. 226.

32 Gutt, *Translation and Relevance*, p. 225.

33 Indeed, it must be noted that from the point of view of the audience, the act of communication actually takes place between the interpreter and the audience, because the text they listen to is produced by the interpreter.

34 T. Ensink, 'The Footing of a Royal Address: An Analysis of Representativeness in Political Speech, Exemplified in Queen Beatrix' Address to the Knesset on March 28, 1995', in *Analysing Political Speeches*, ed. C. Schäffner (Clevedon–Philadelphia–Toronto–Sydney–Johannesburg: Multilingual Matters Ltd, 1997), pp. 5–32 (p. 24).

35 The Italian and British peoples can be considered part of the audience because they participate in the event through its reporting in the press.

36 More specifically, the English interpreter should bear in mind that President Ciampi is an ardent supporter of the European Union and that he has tried to revive patriotic feelings on the domestic front.

37 Anaphora is the repetition of a word or phrase in successive clauses. Cataphora describes the relation between an anaphoric expression and an 'antecedent' that comes later.

38 N. Zingarelli, *Lo Zingarelli 1994. Vocabolario della lingua italiana* (Bologna: Zanichelli, 1993), p. 782.